SCI-FI COLORING BOOK

SPACE CRAFT

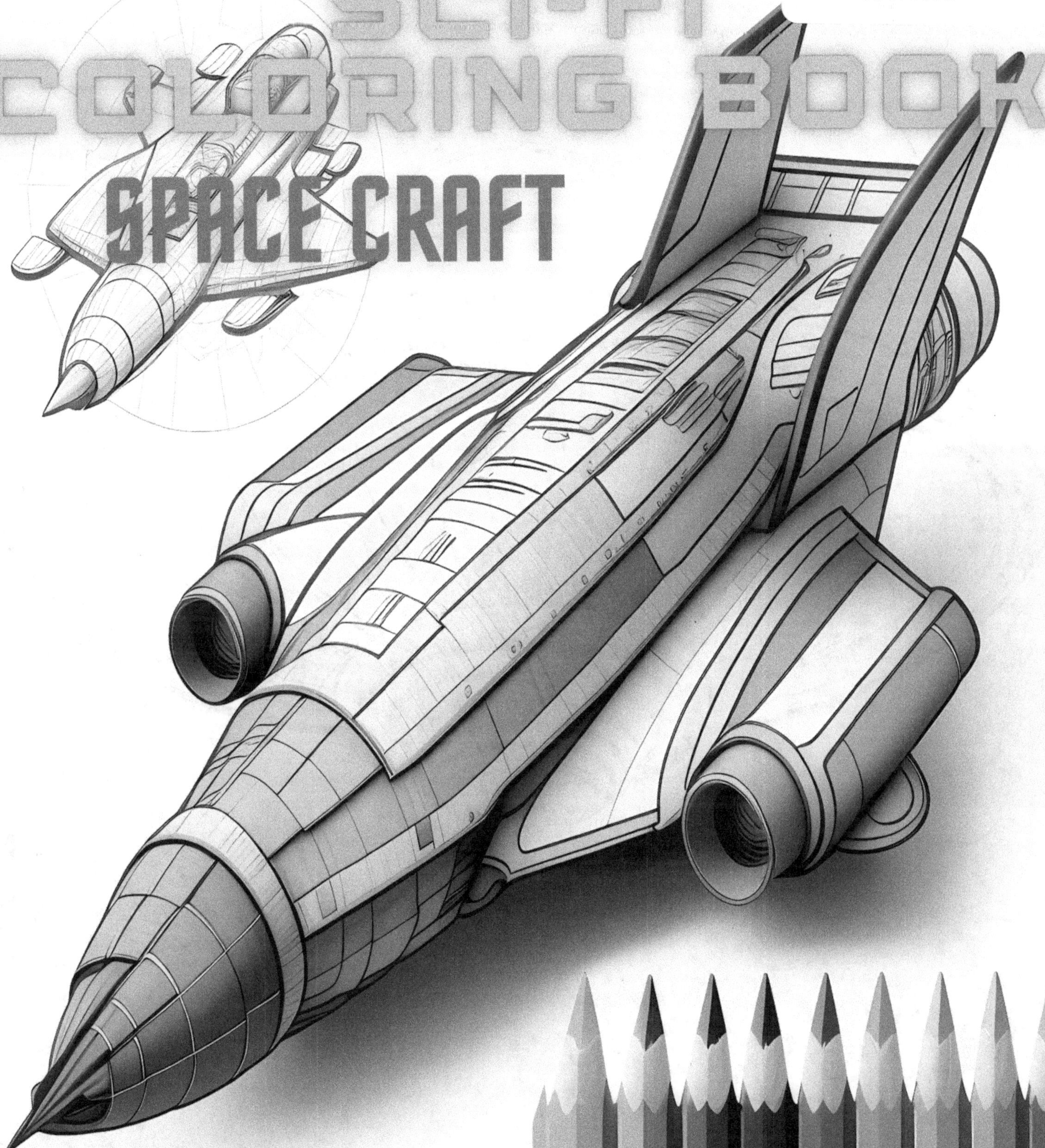

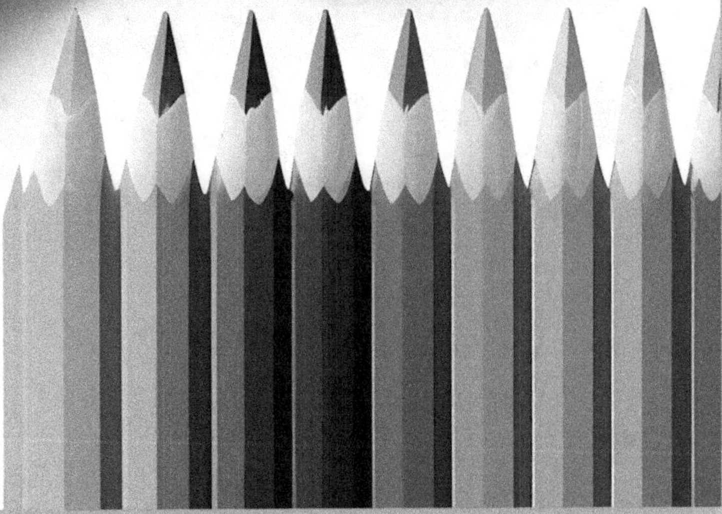

L.A. HOBDAY

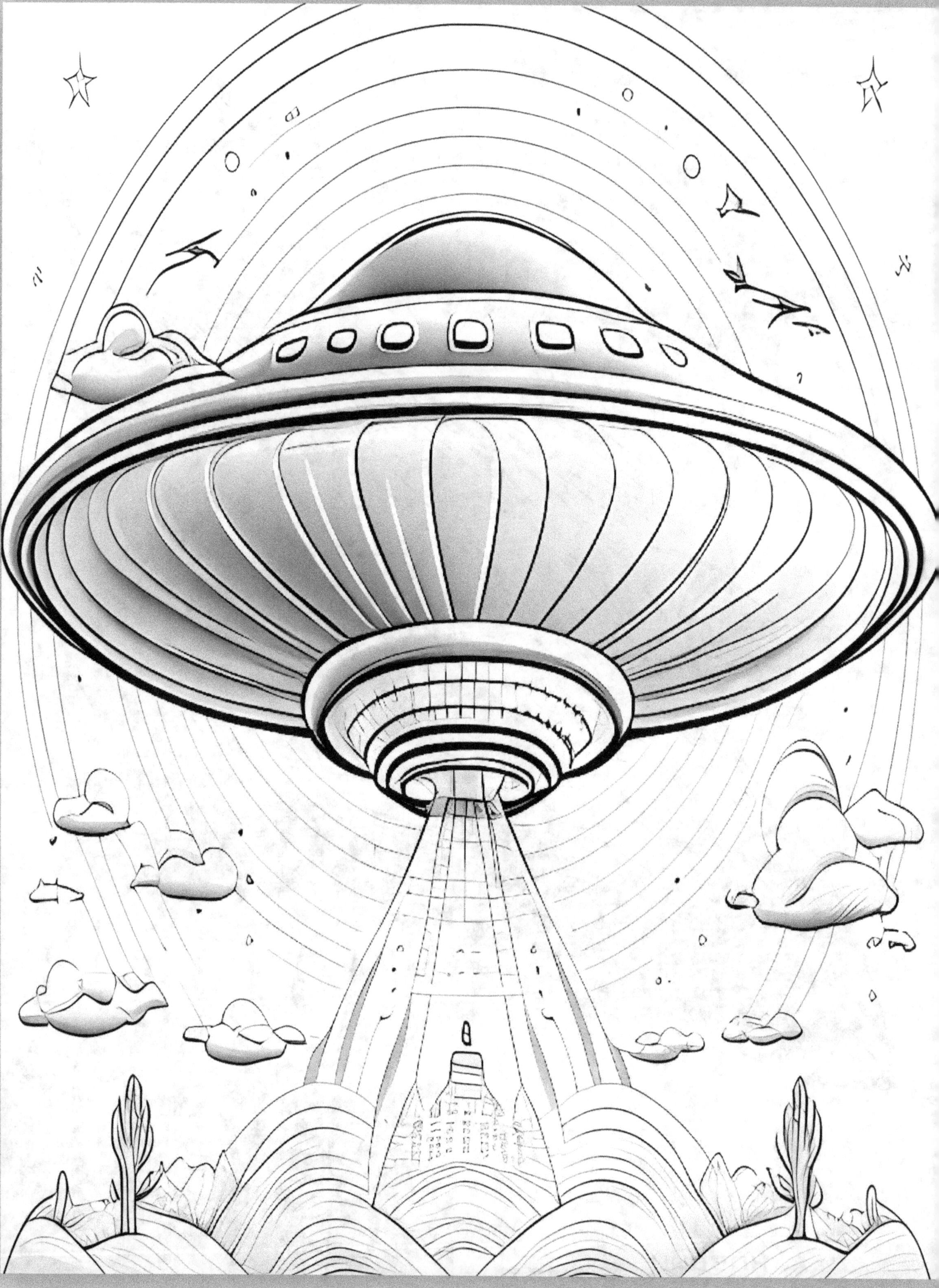

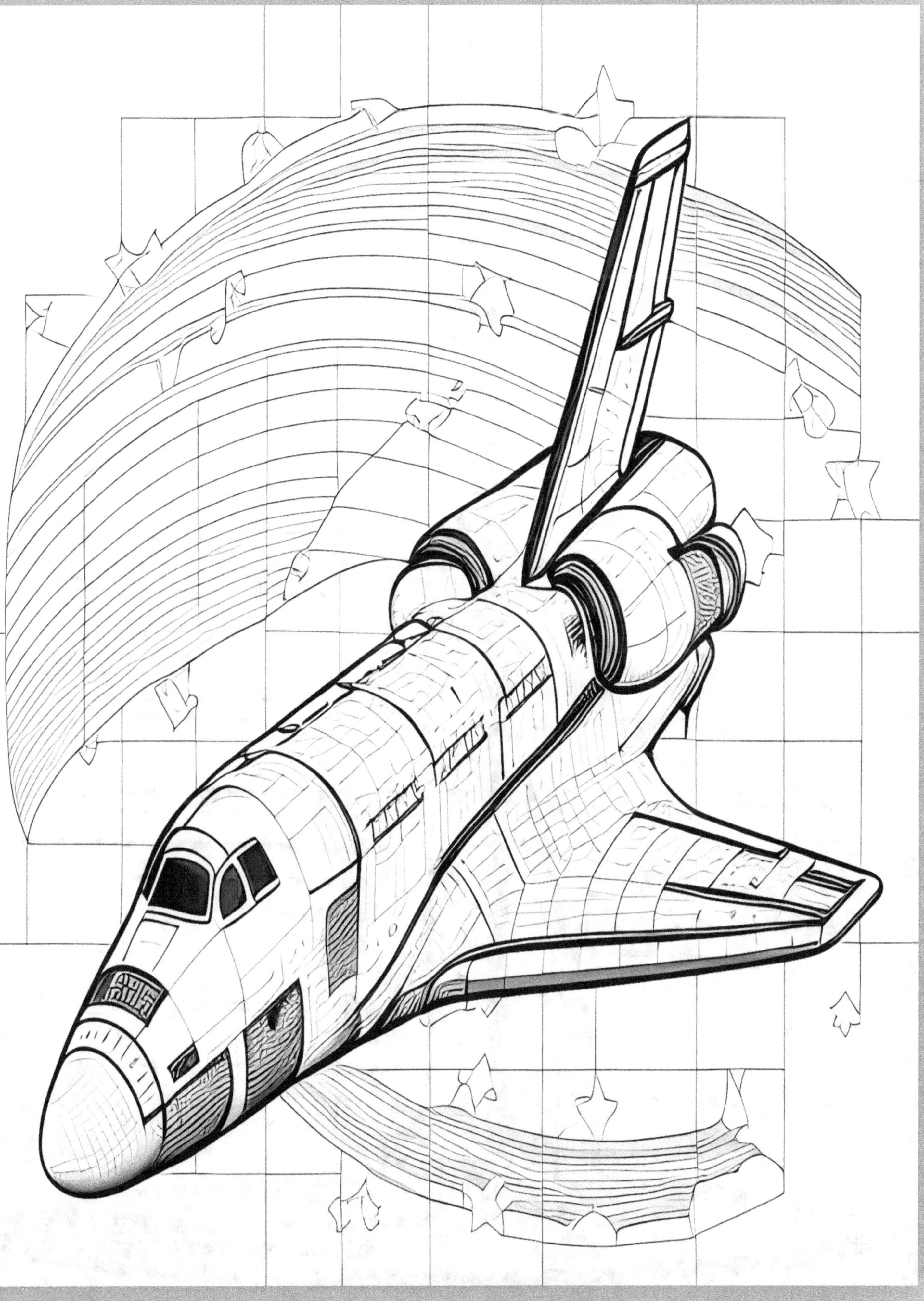

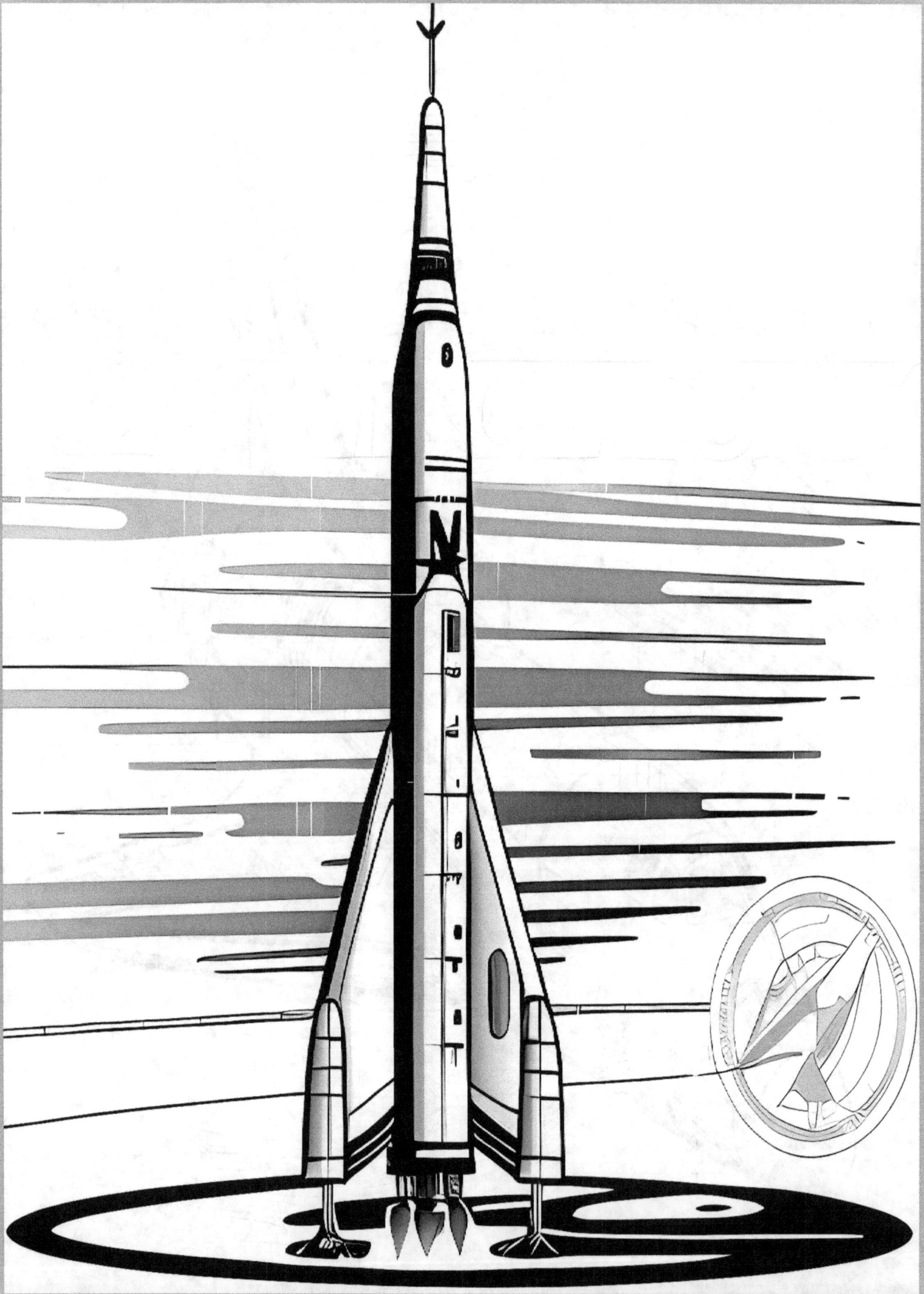

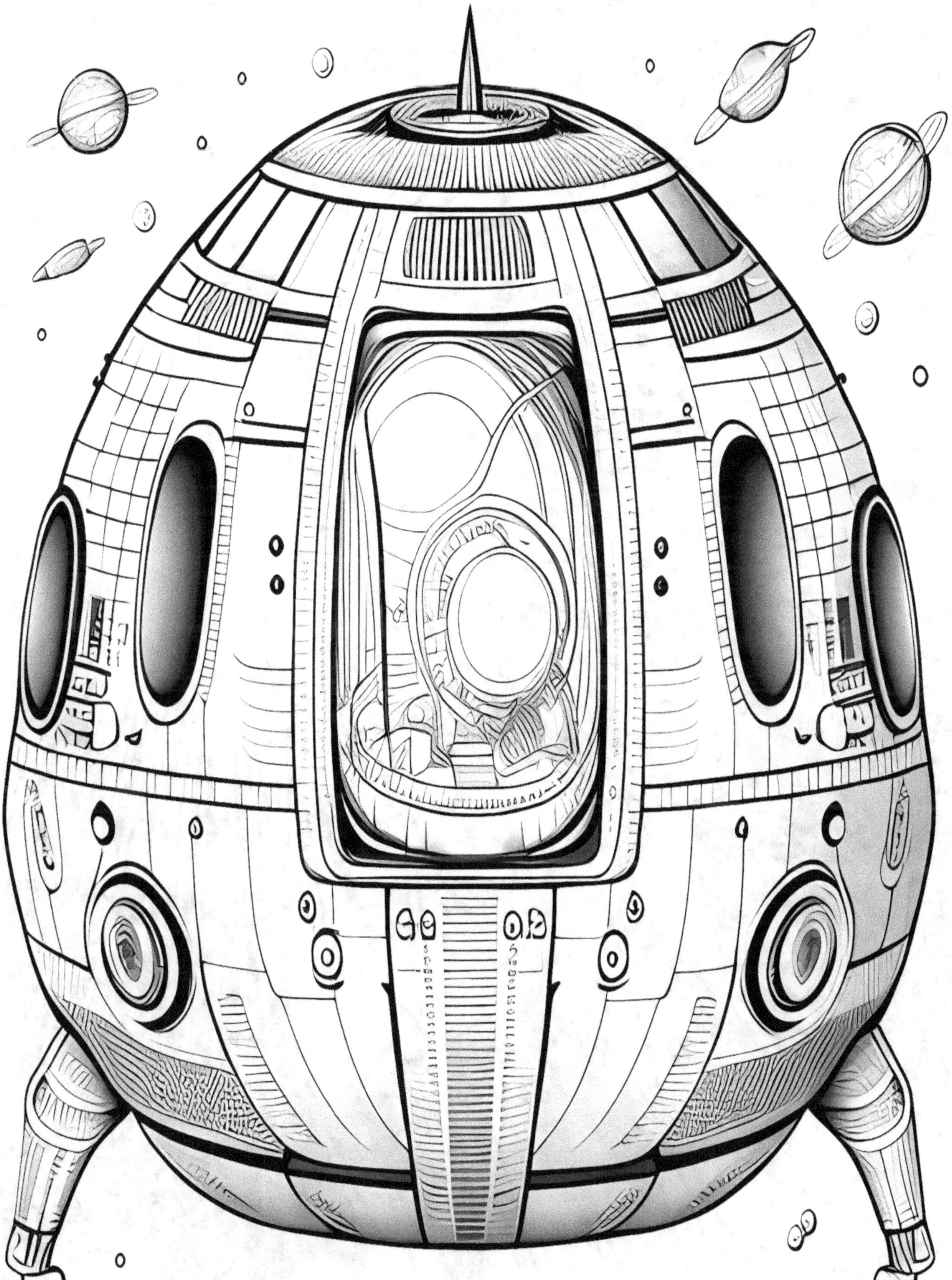

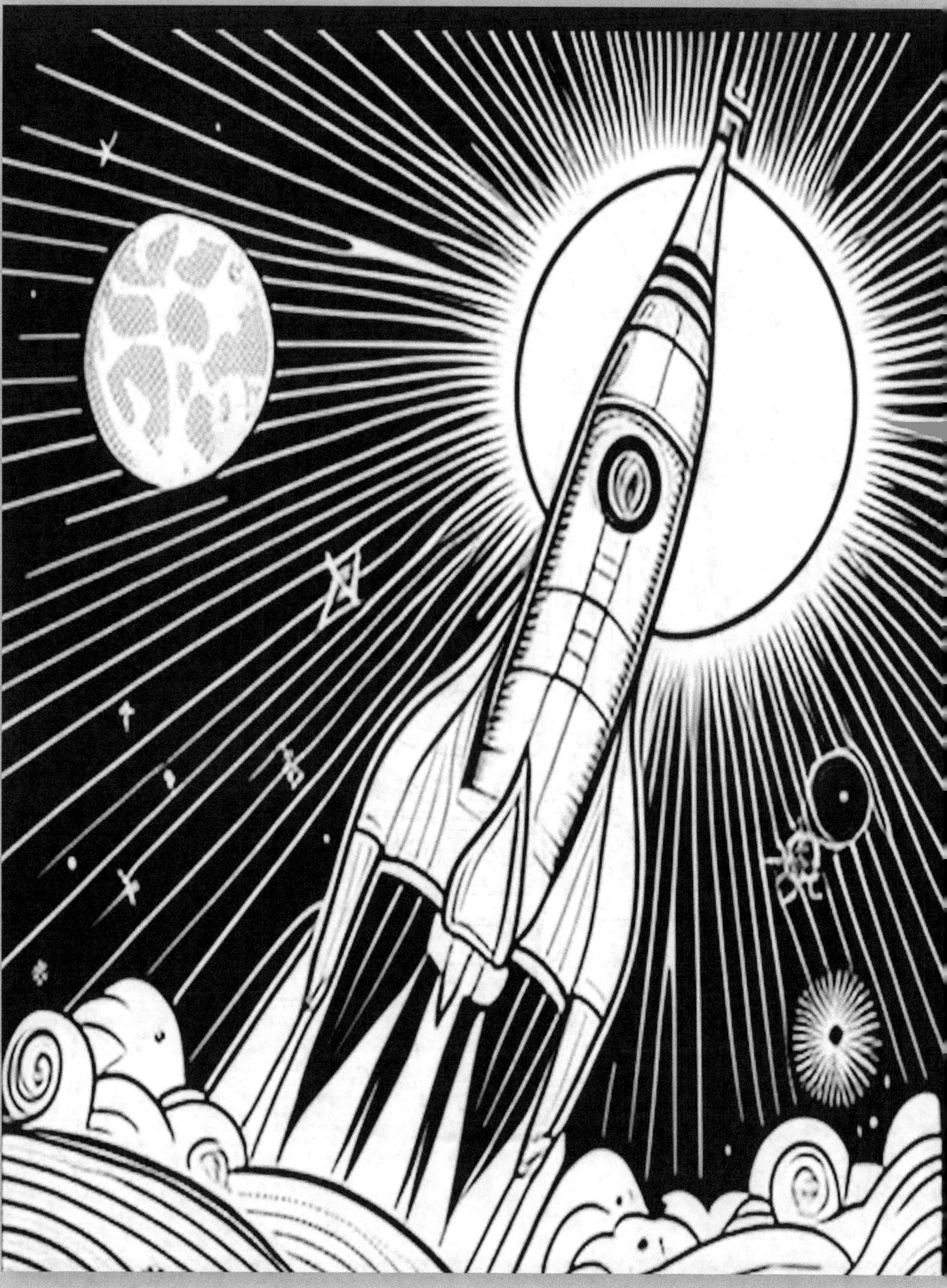

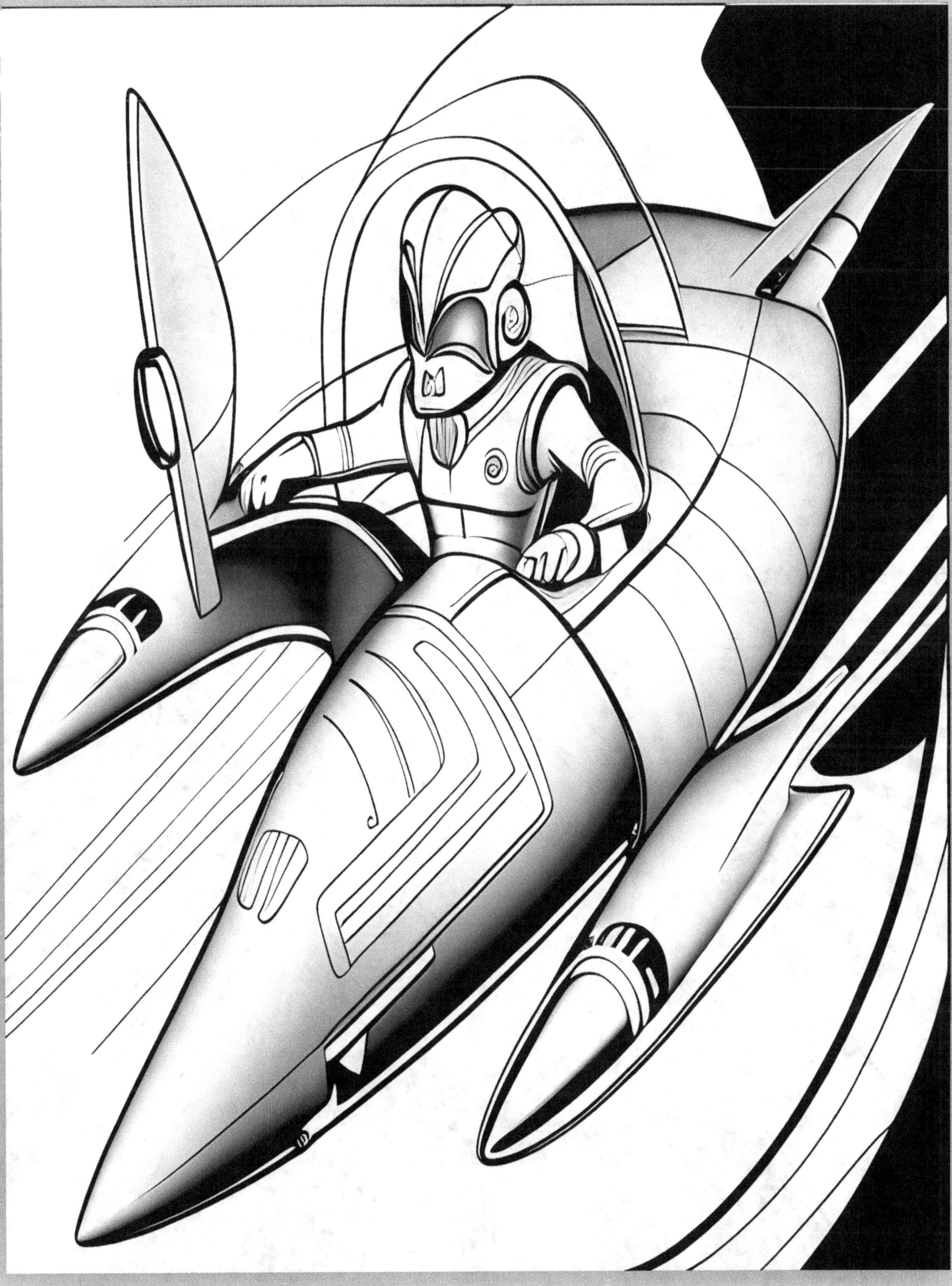

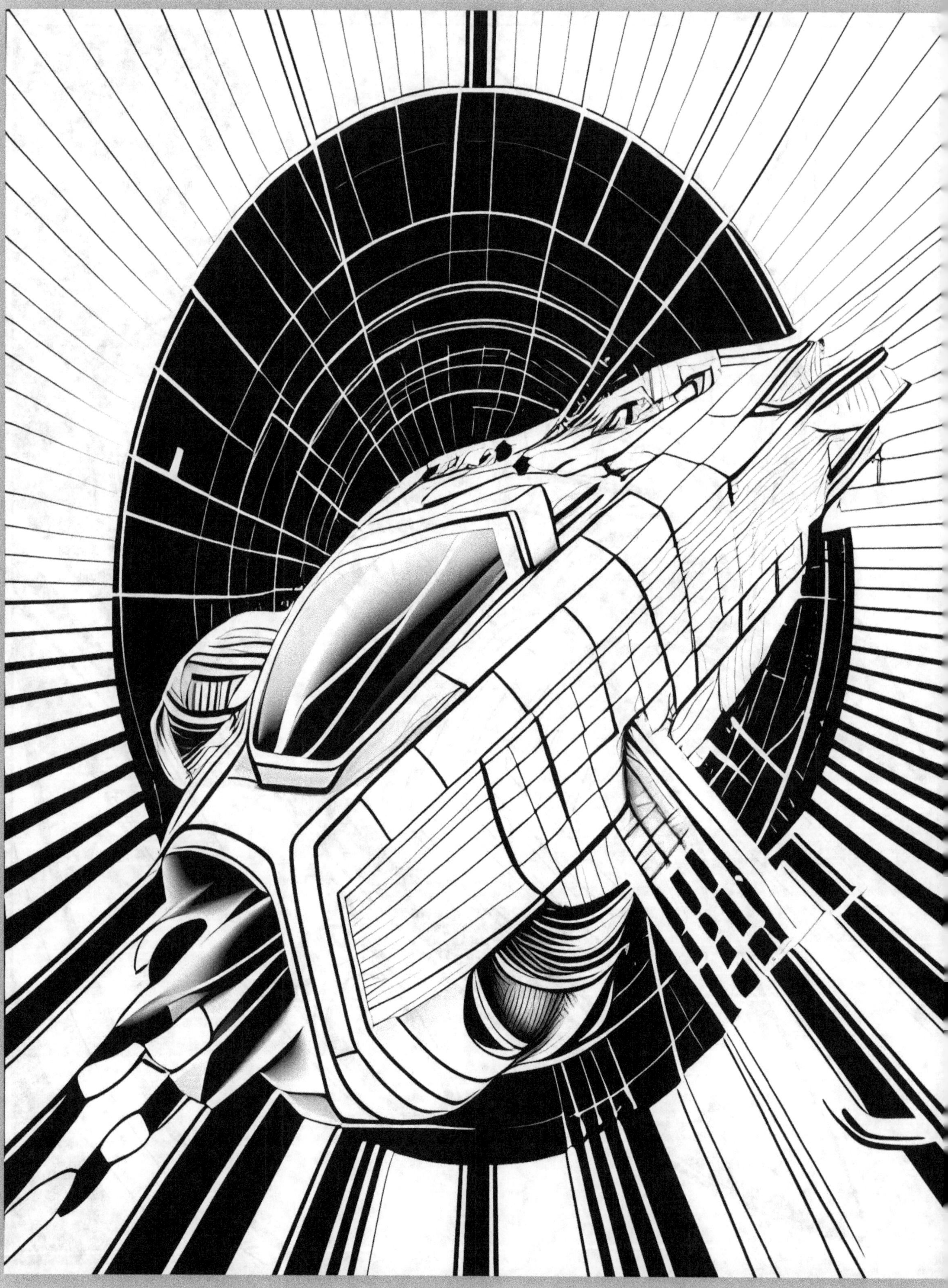

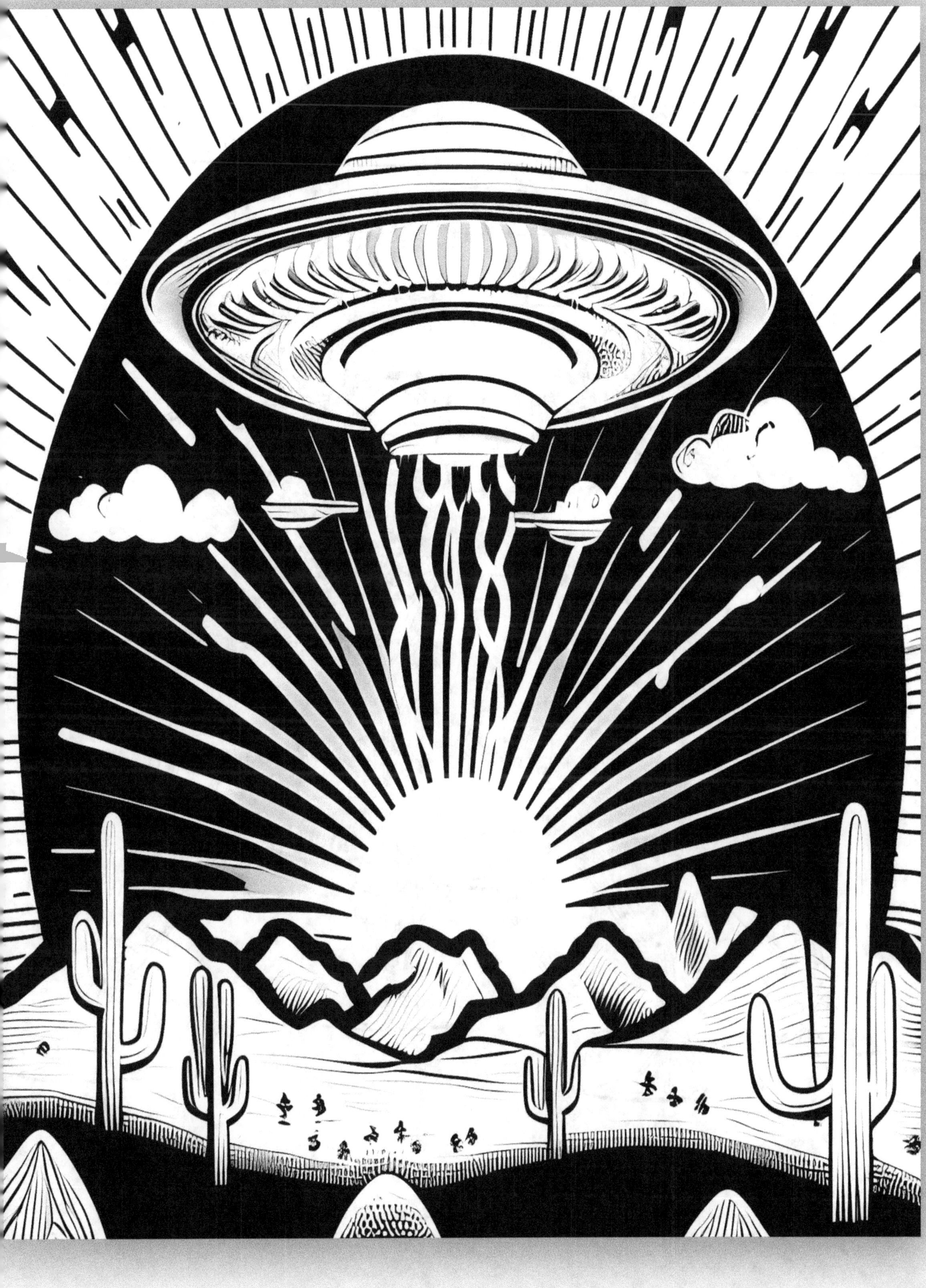

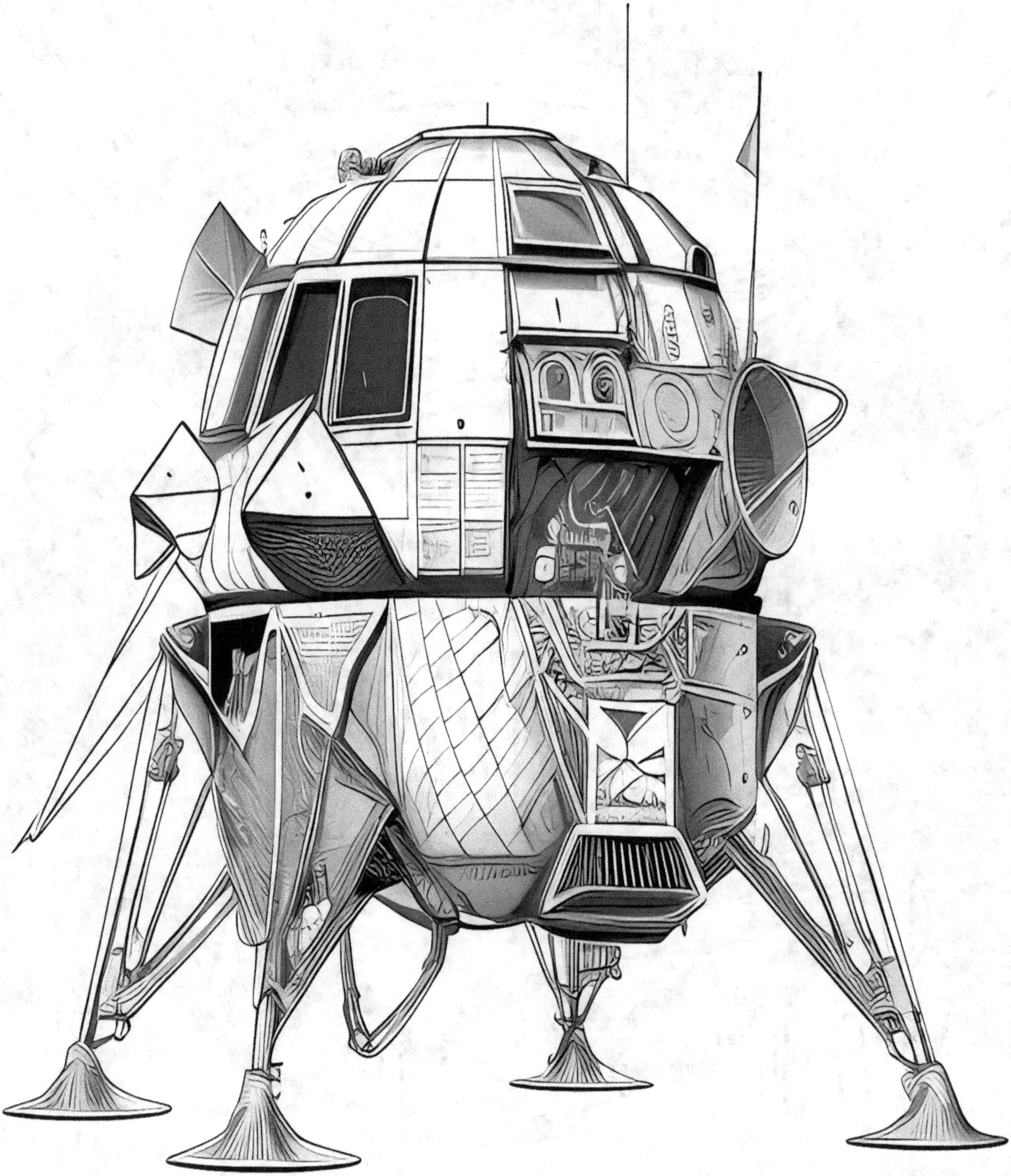

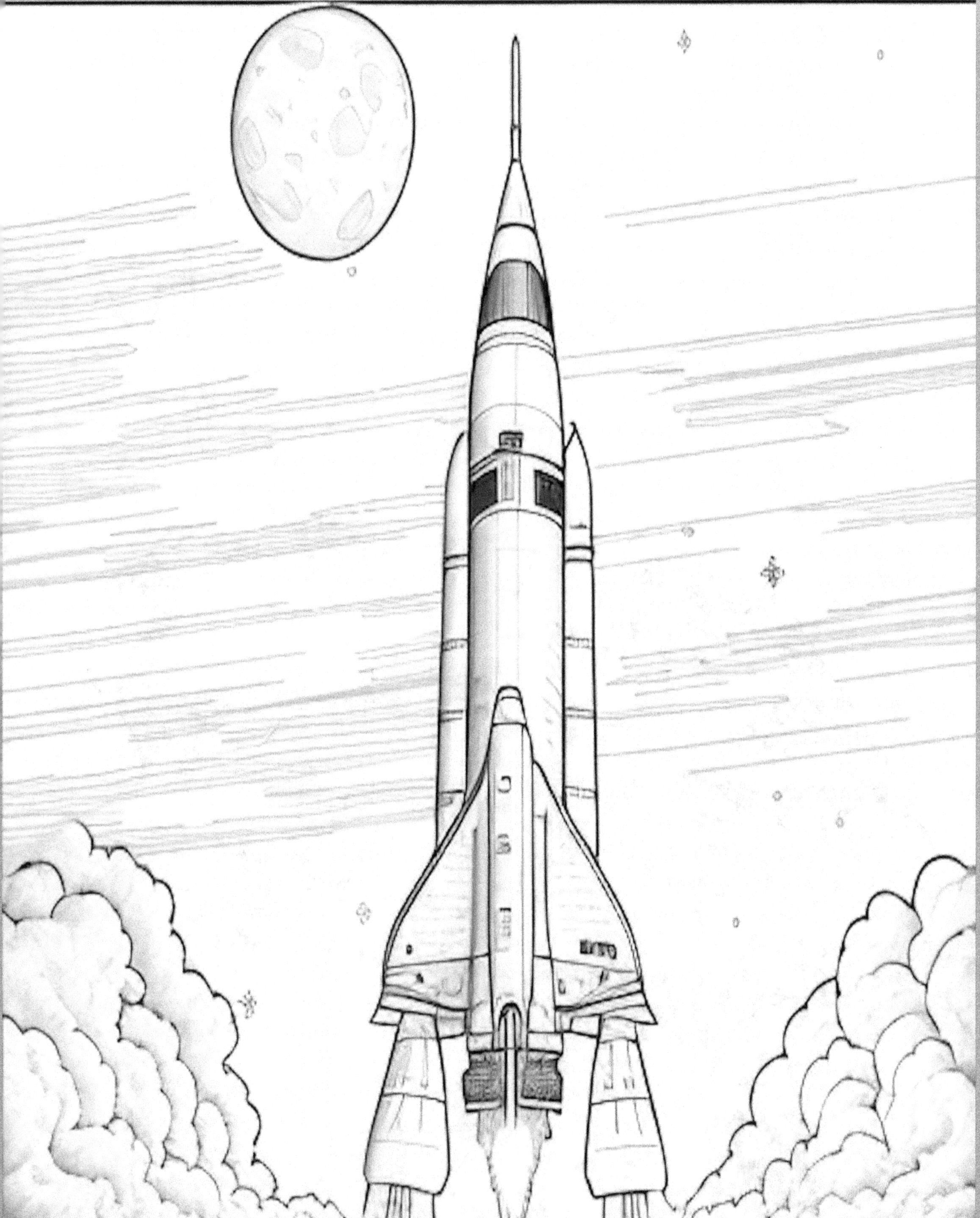

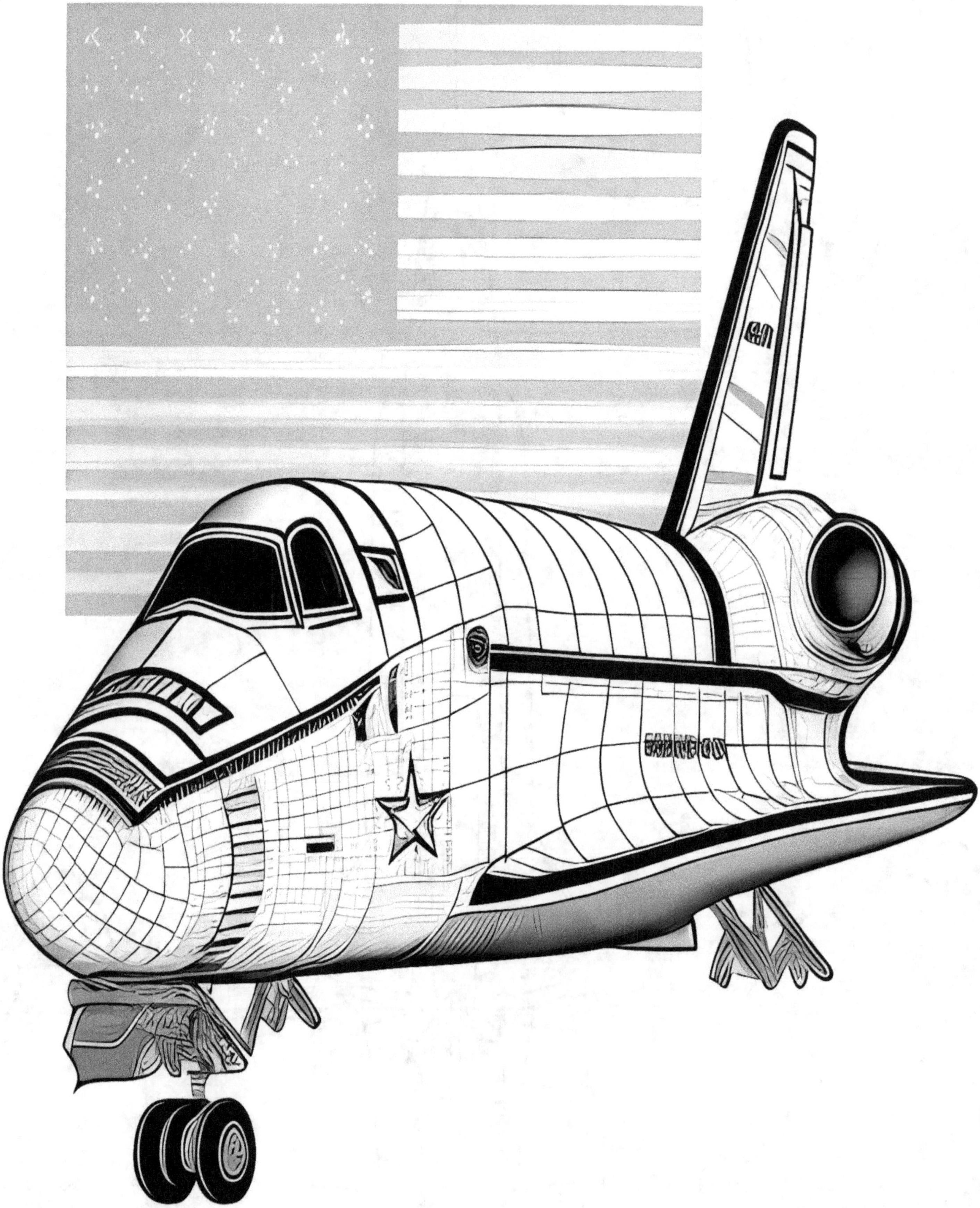

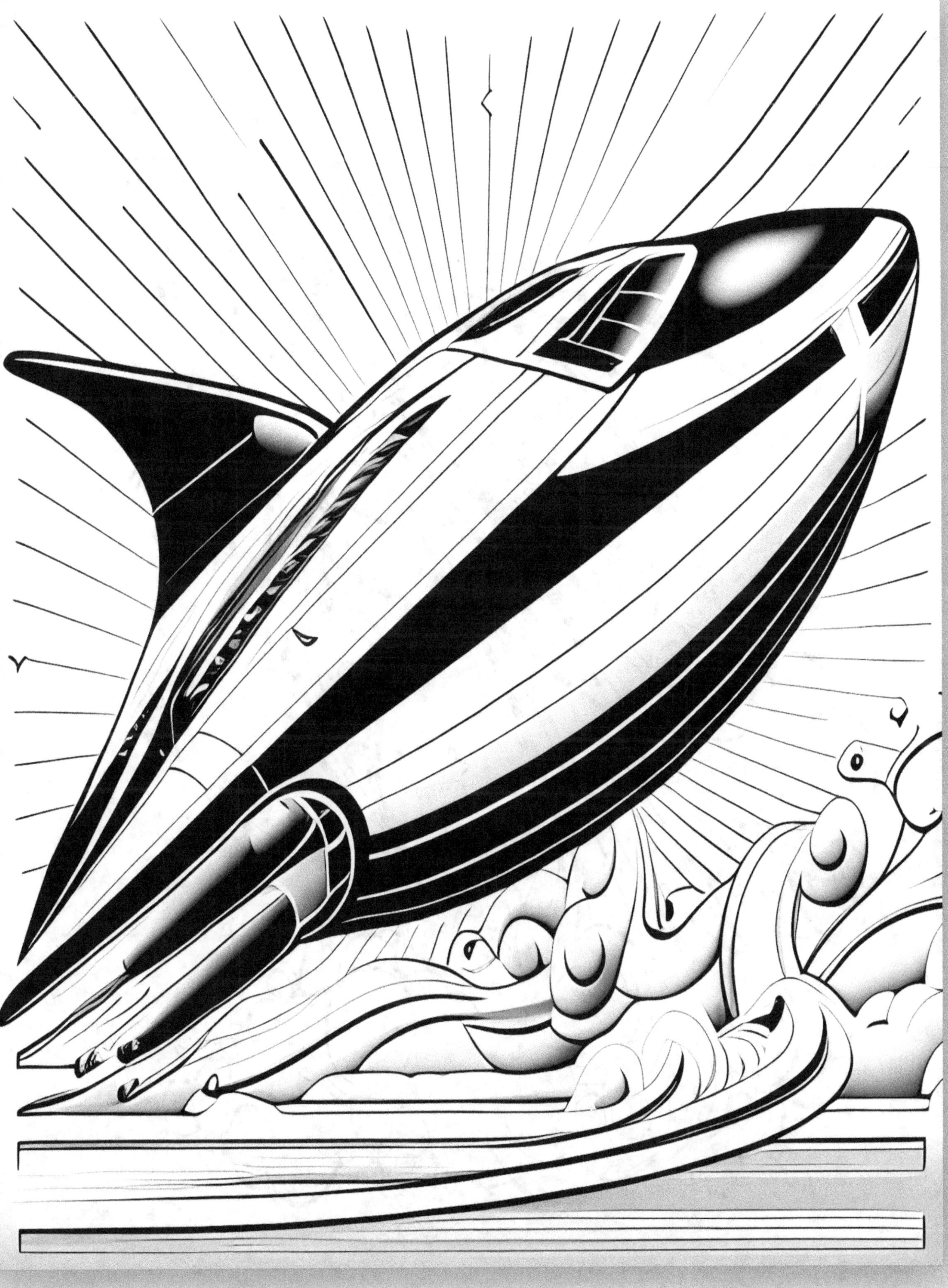

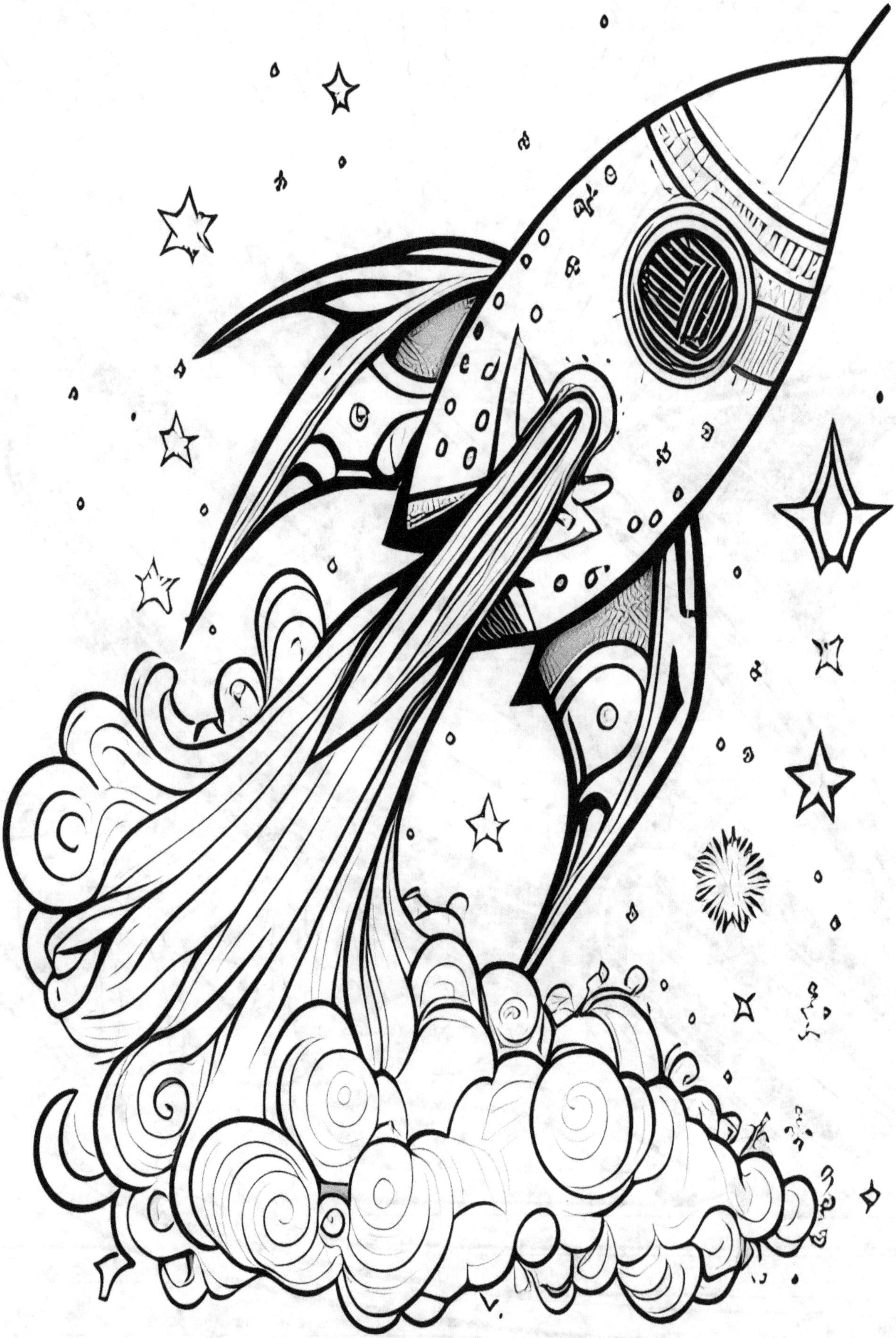

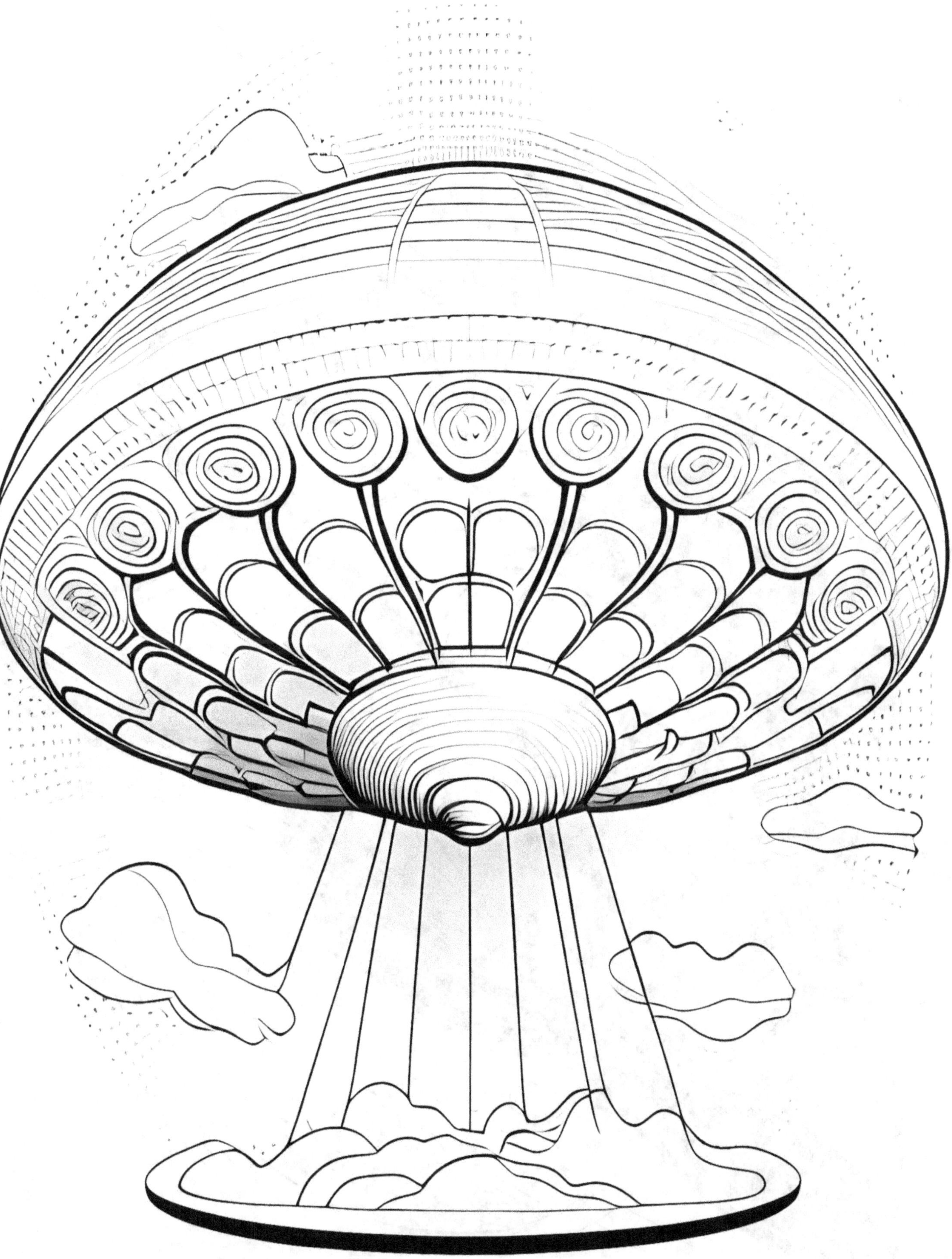

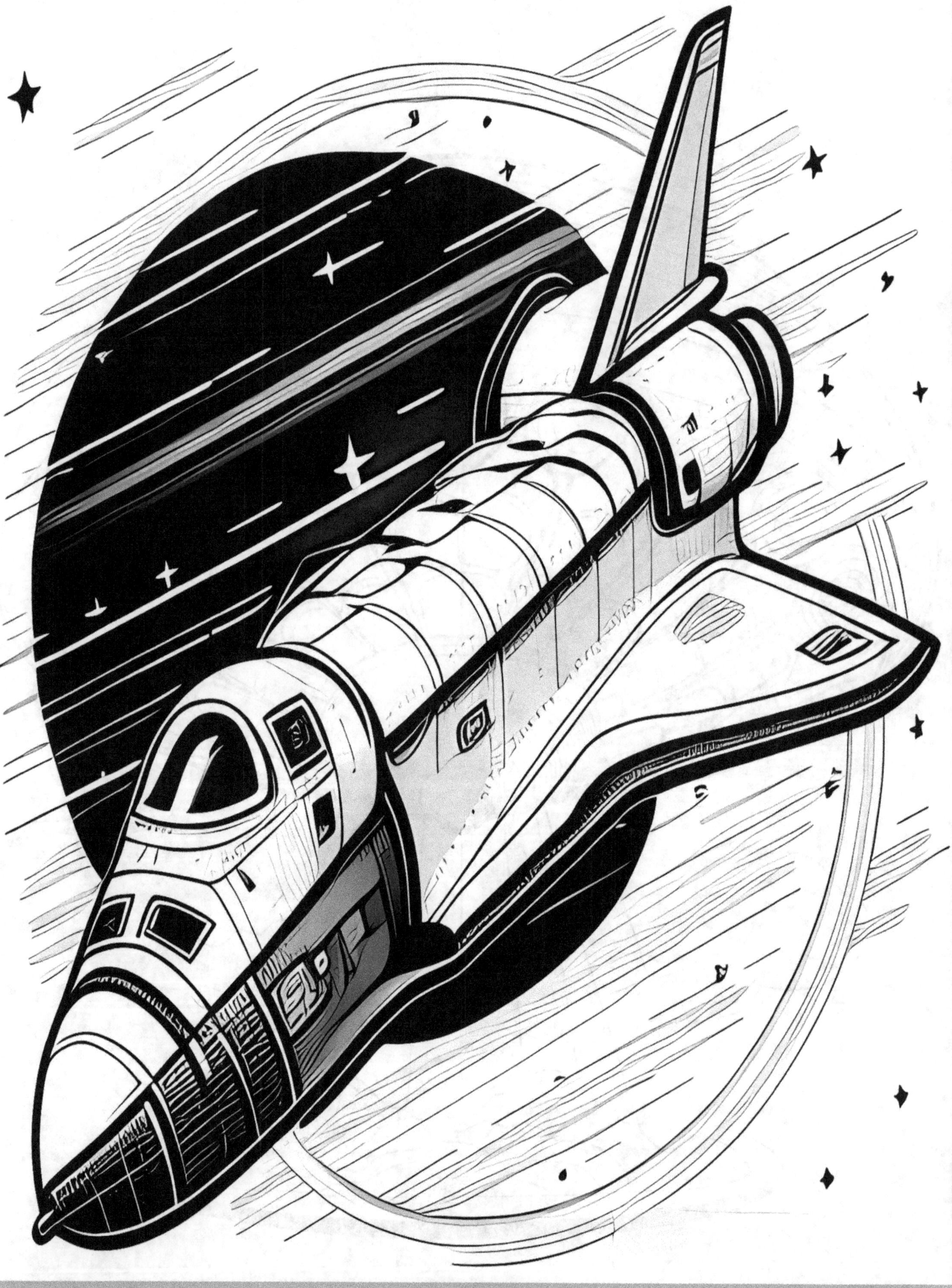

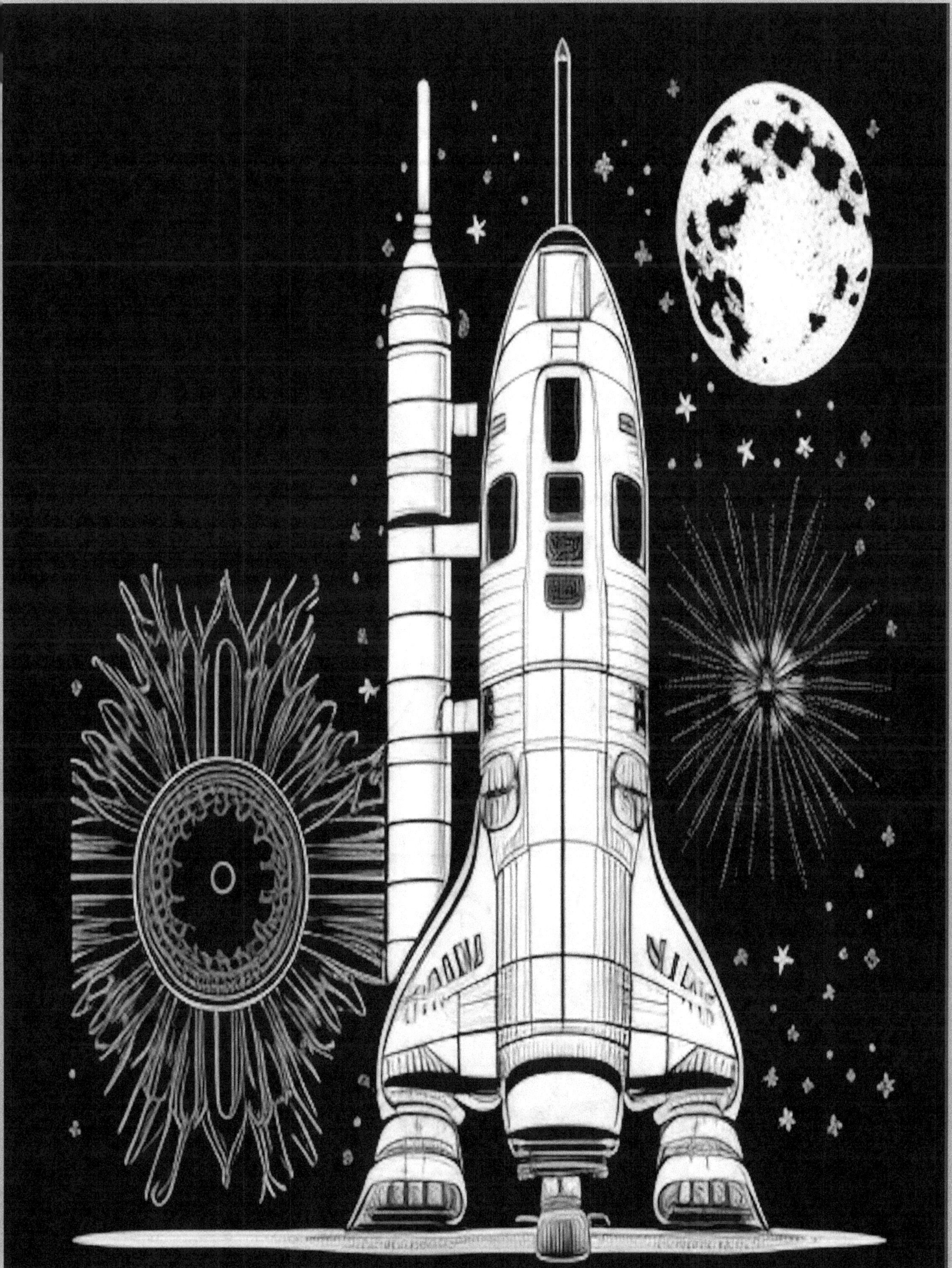

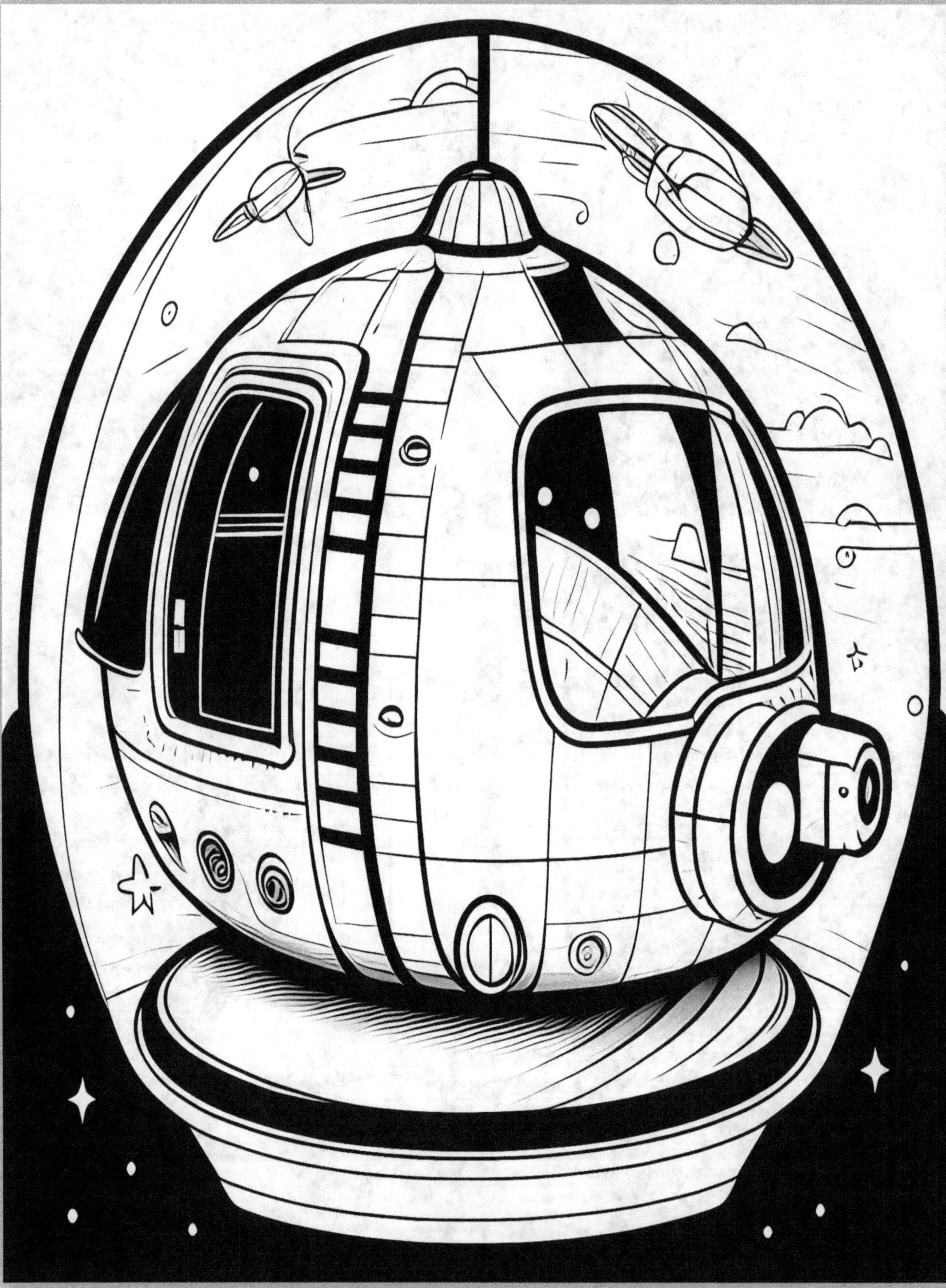

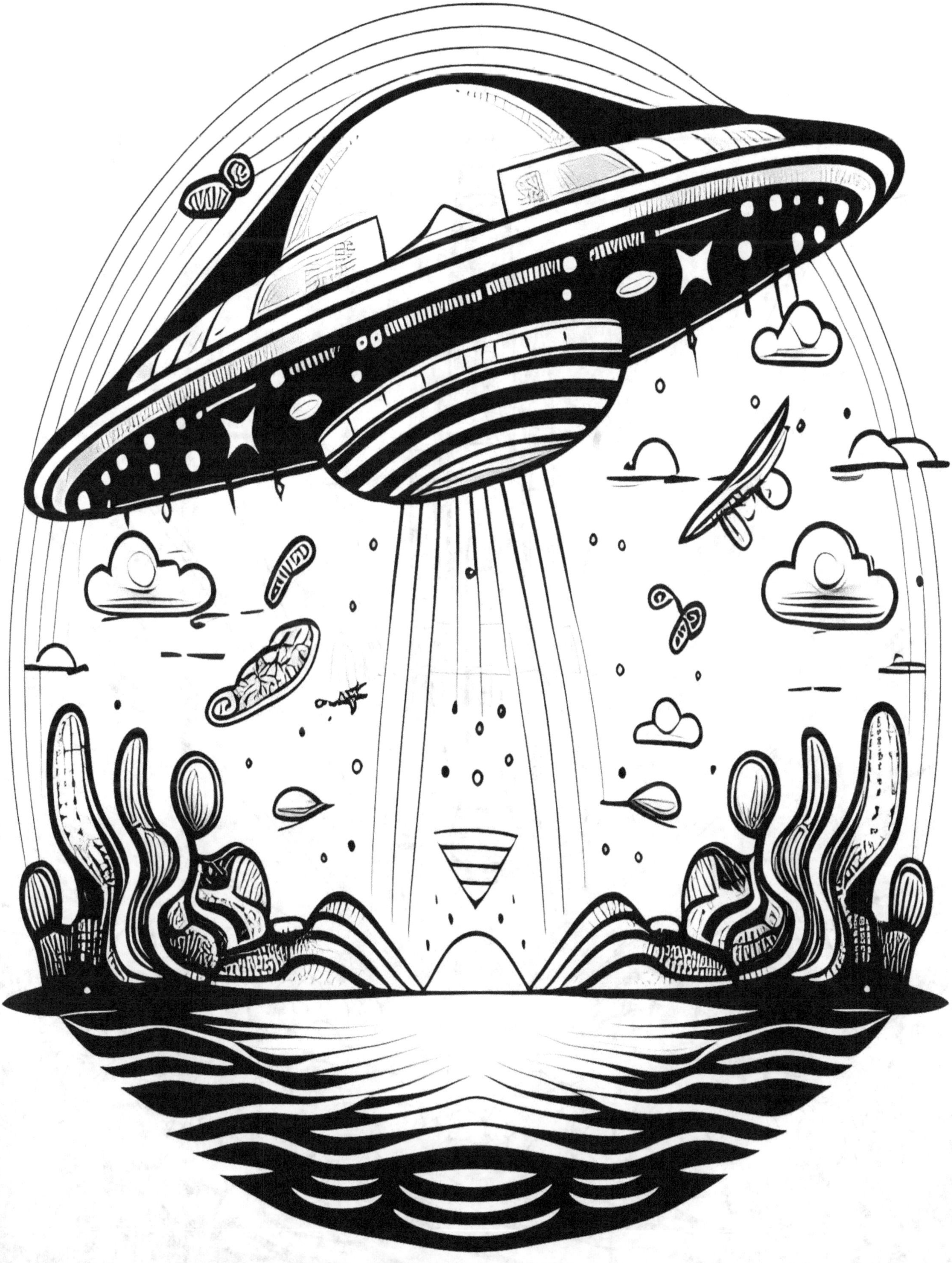

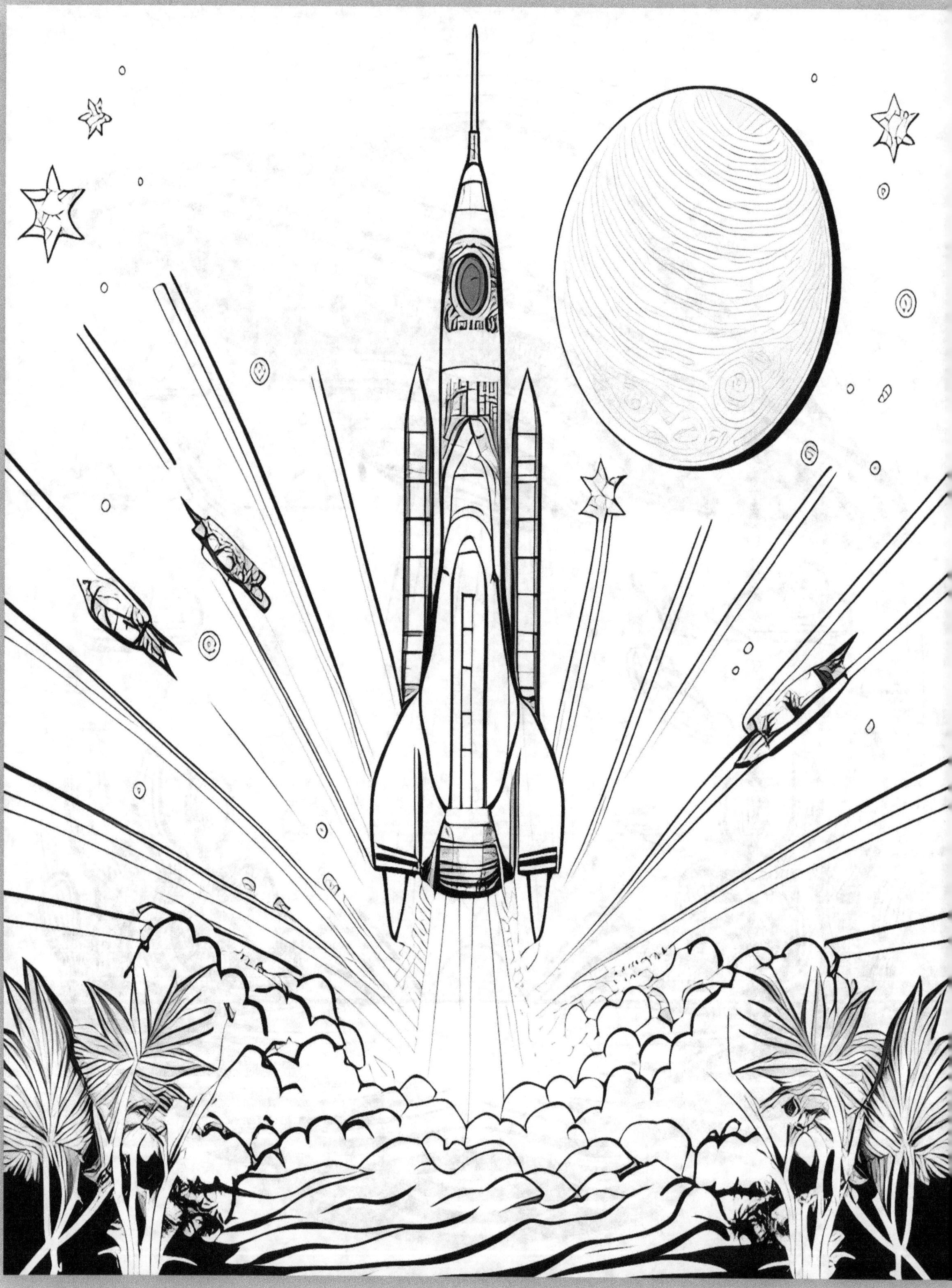

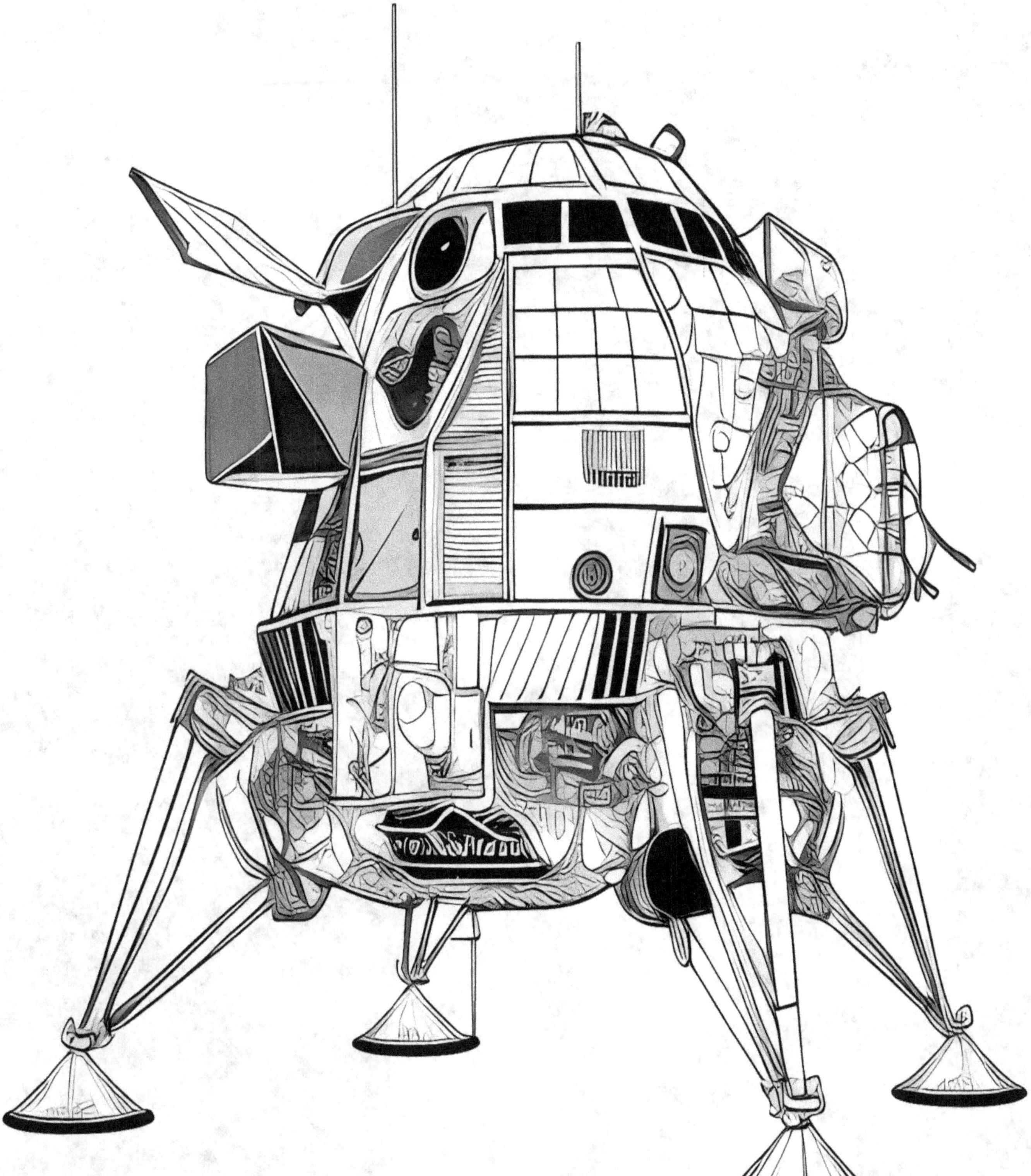

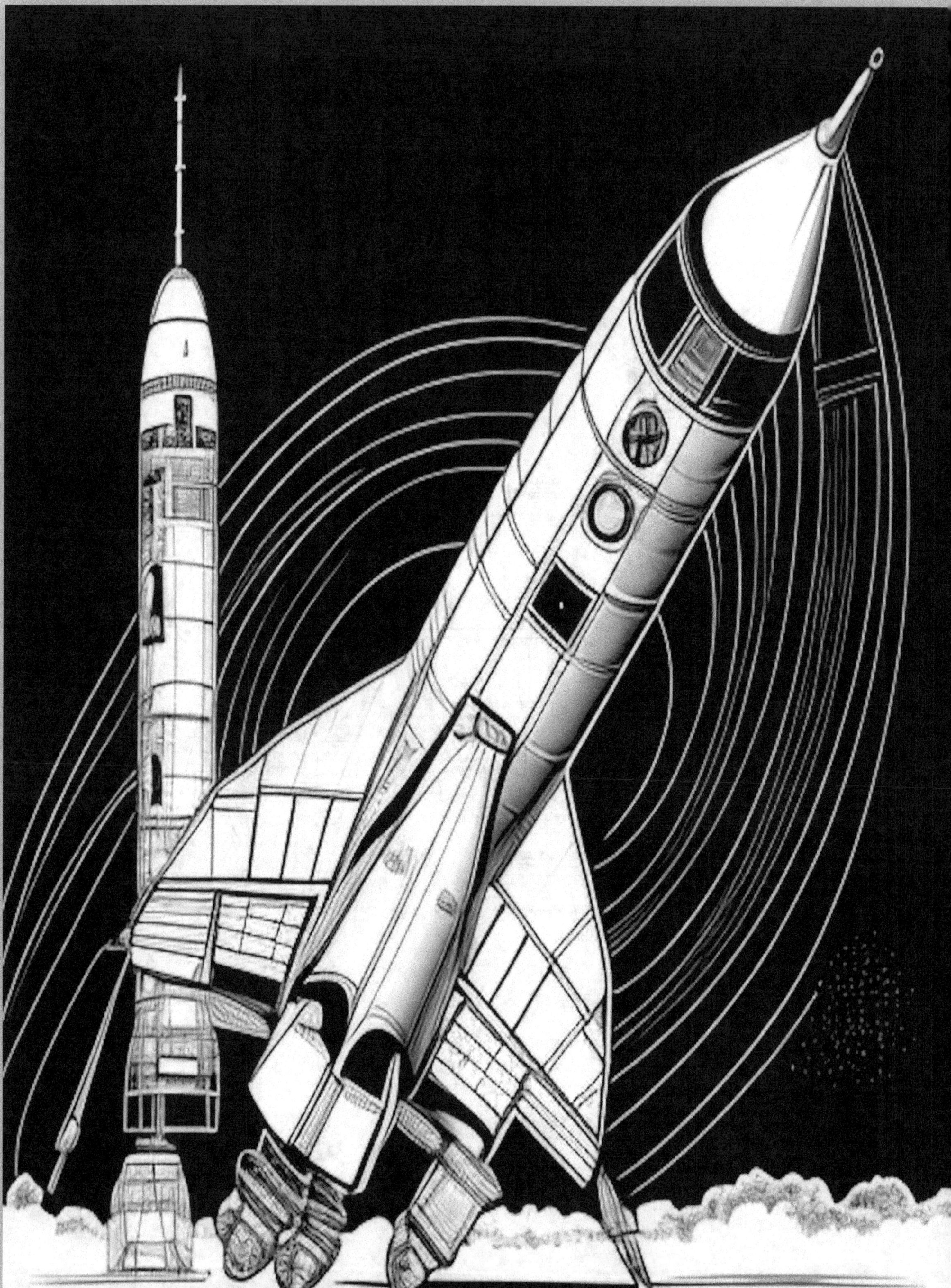

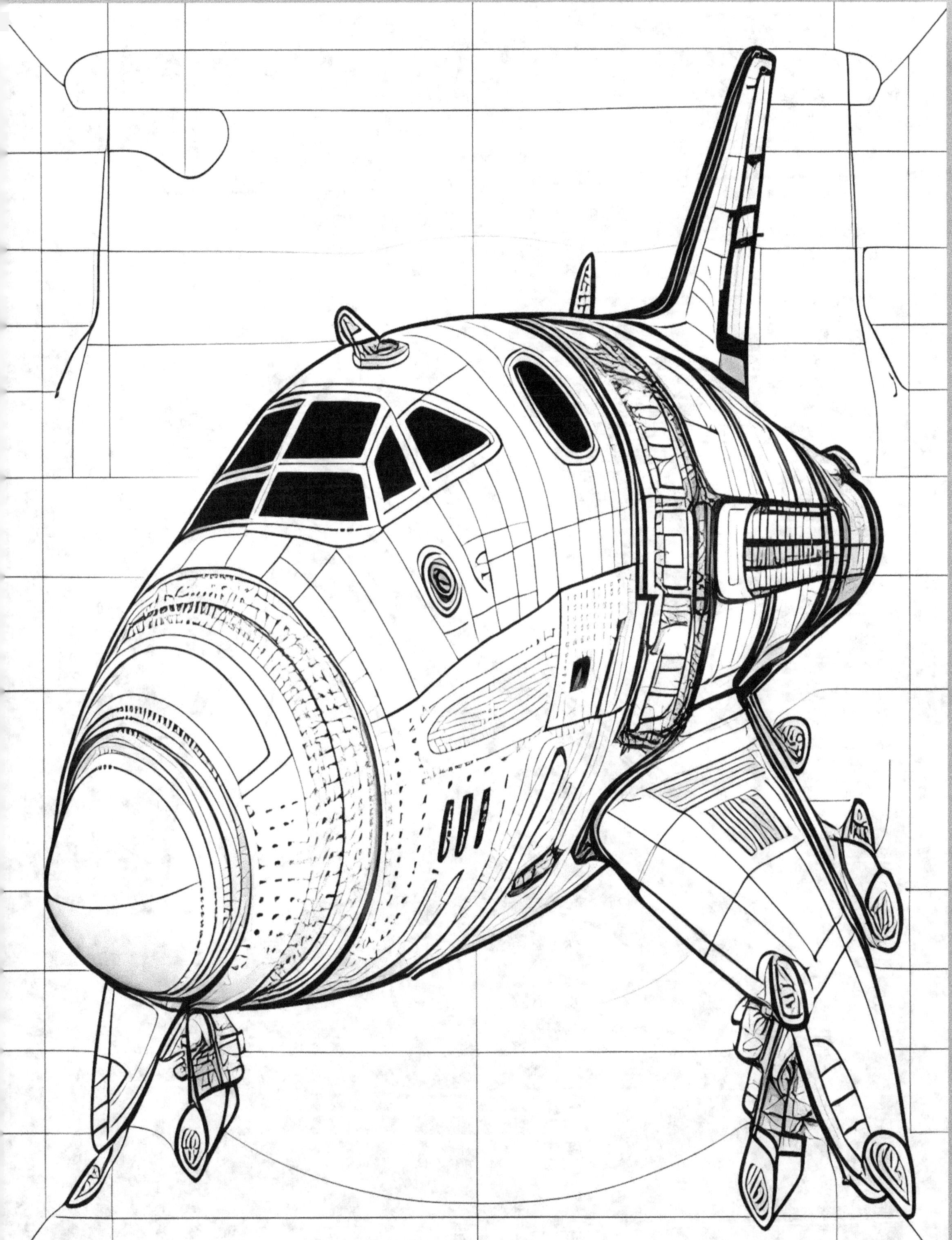

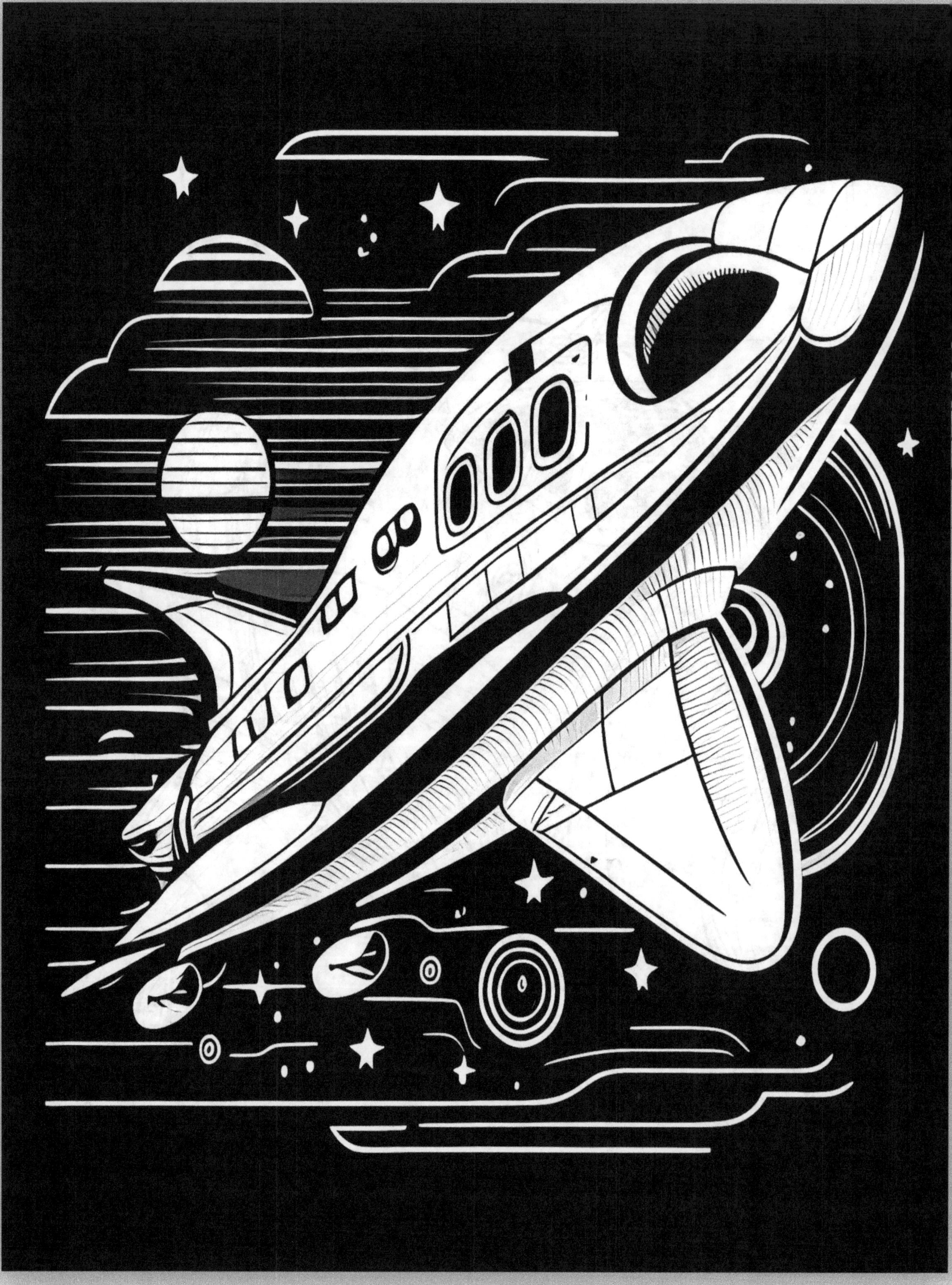

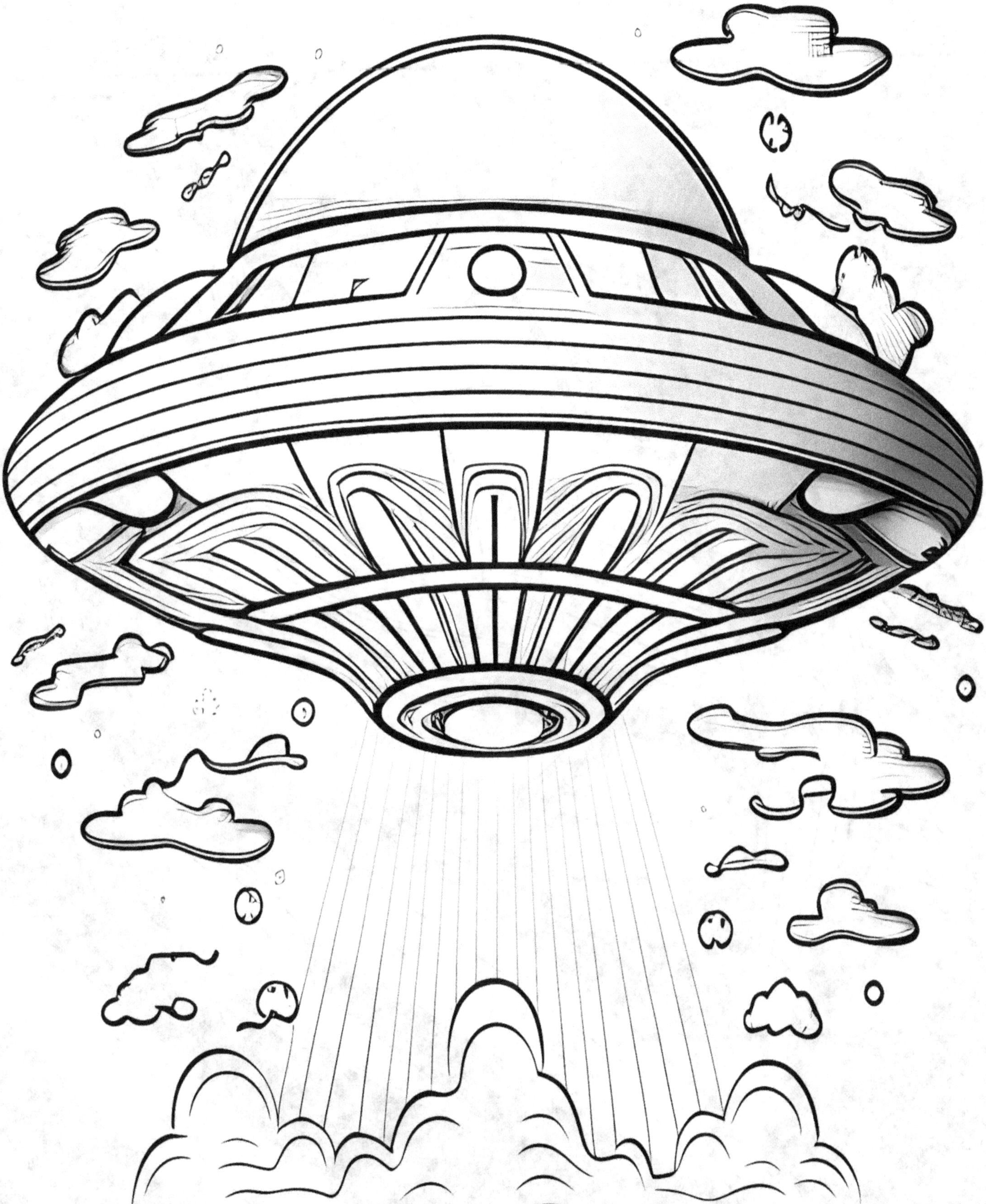

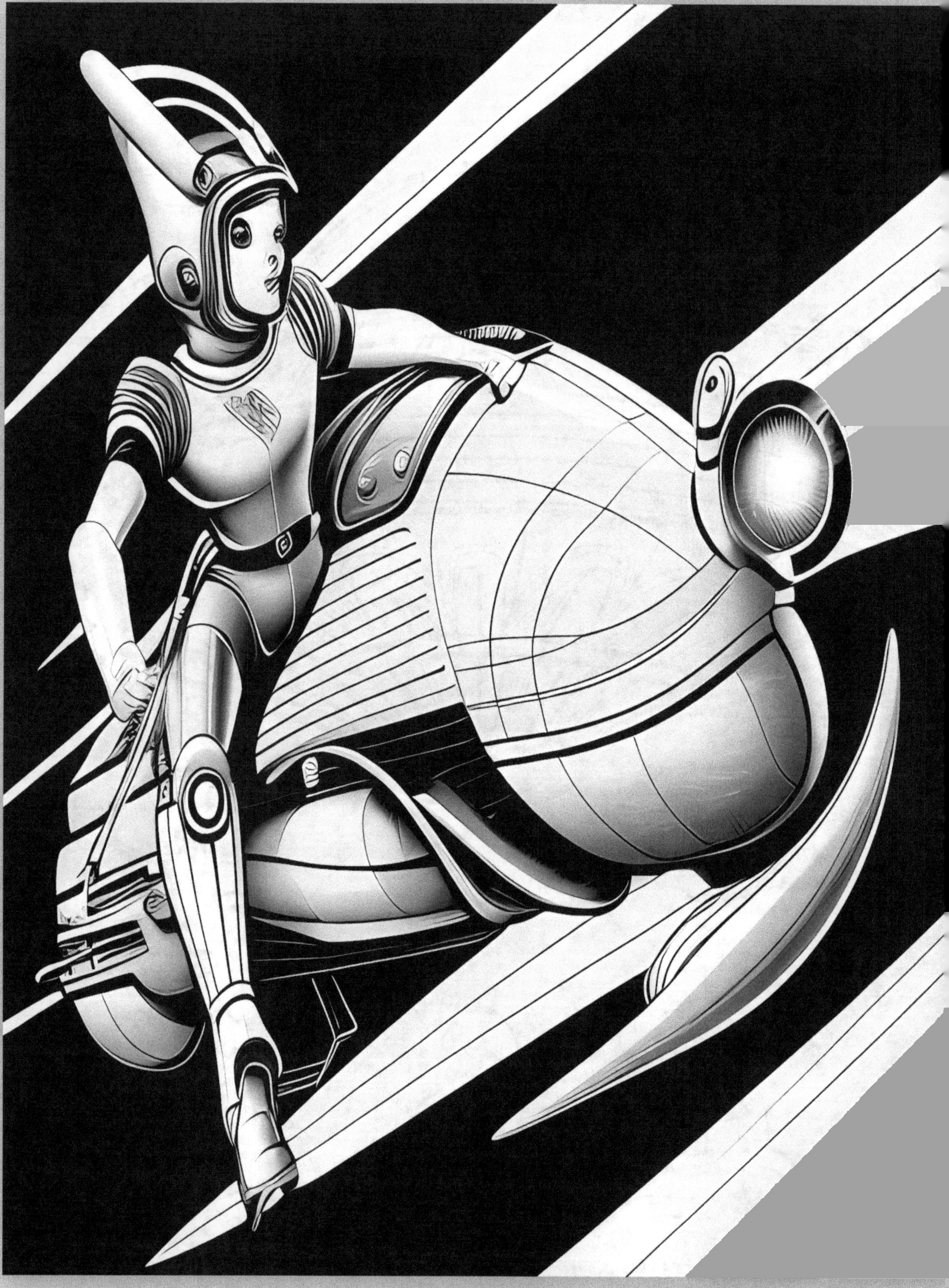

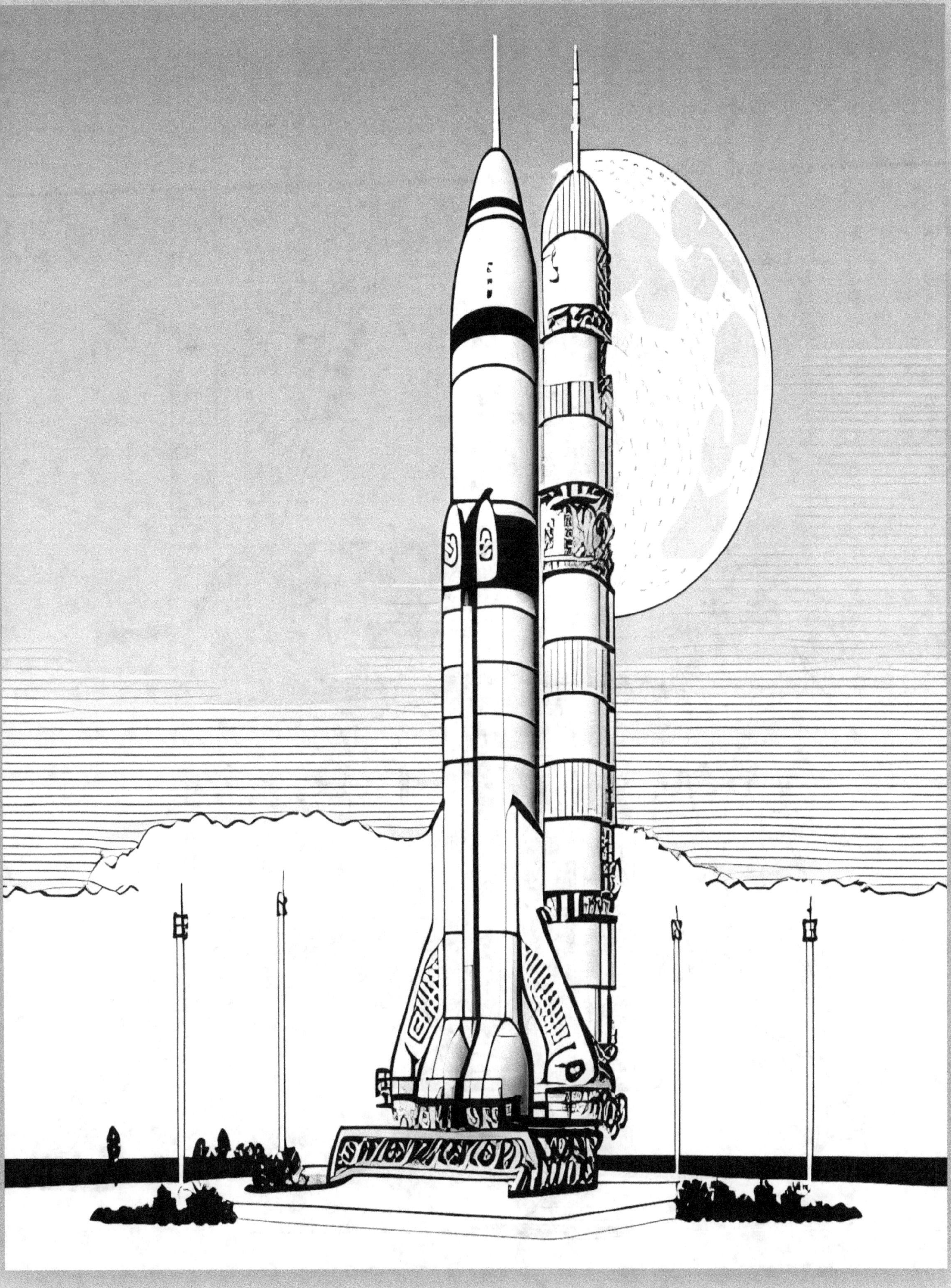

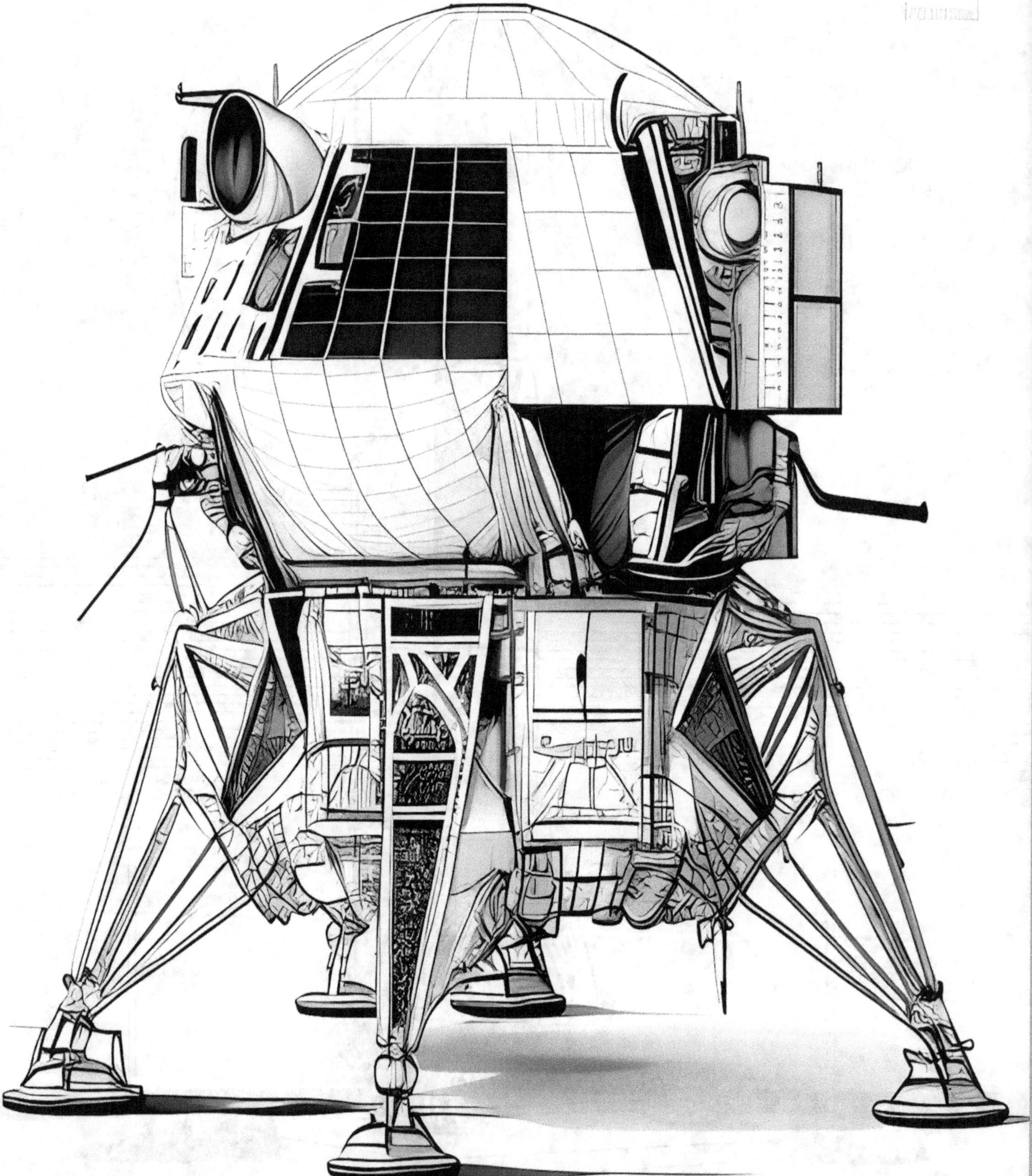

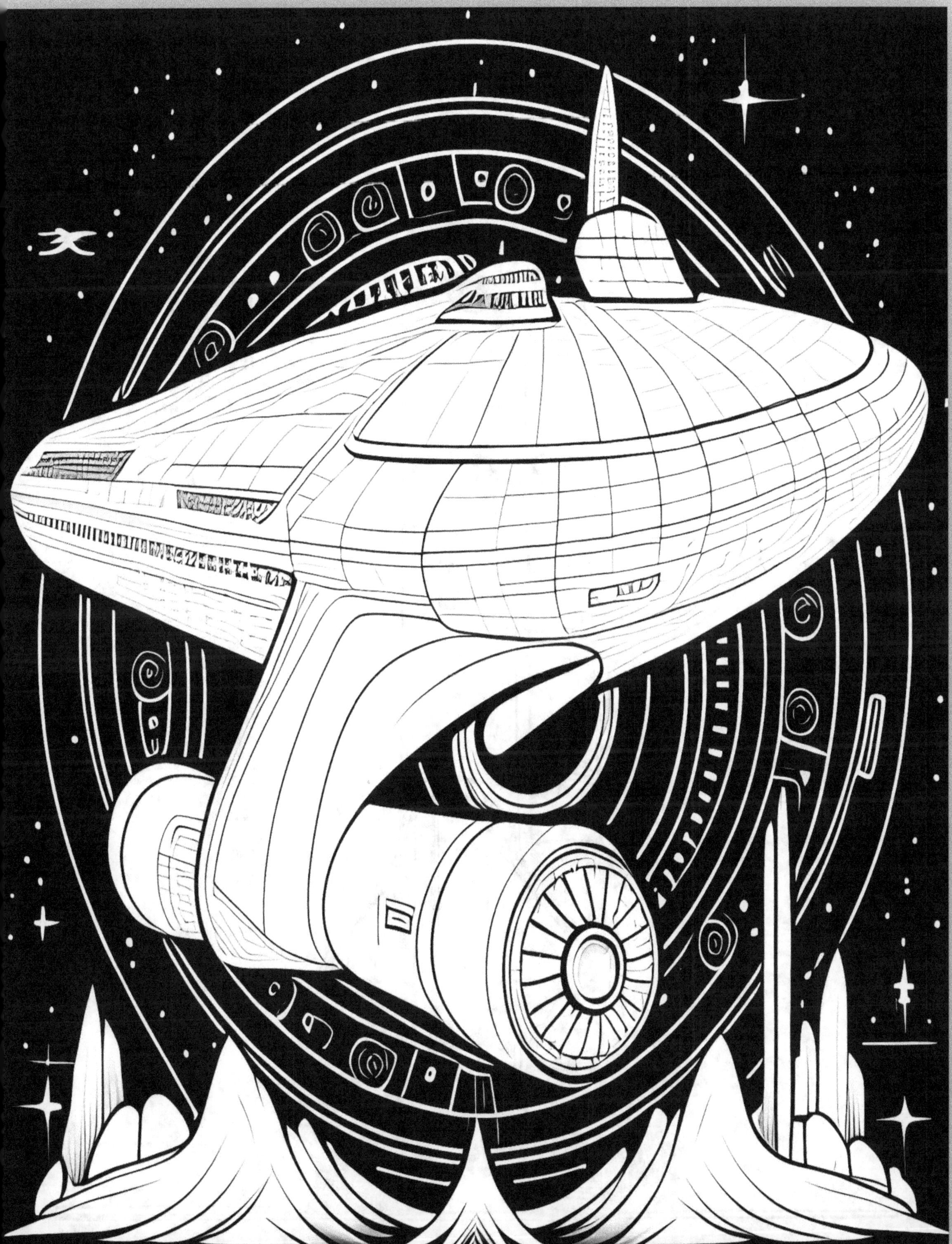

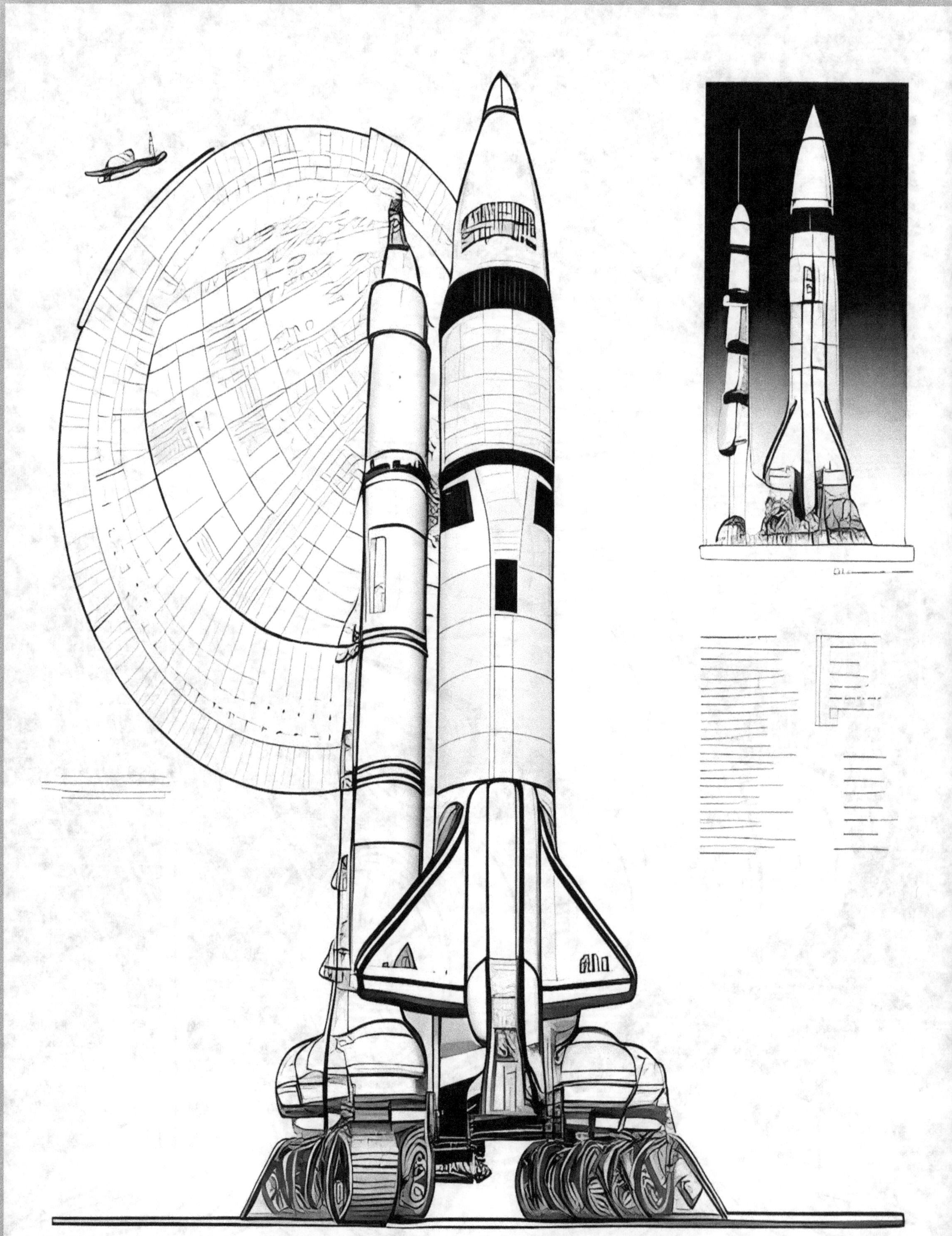

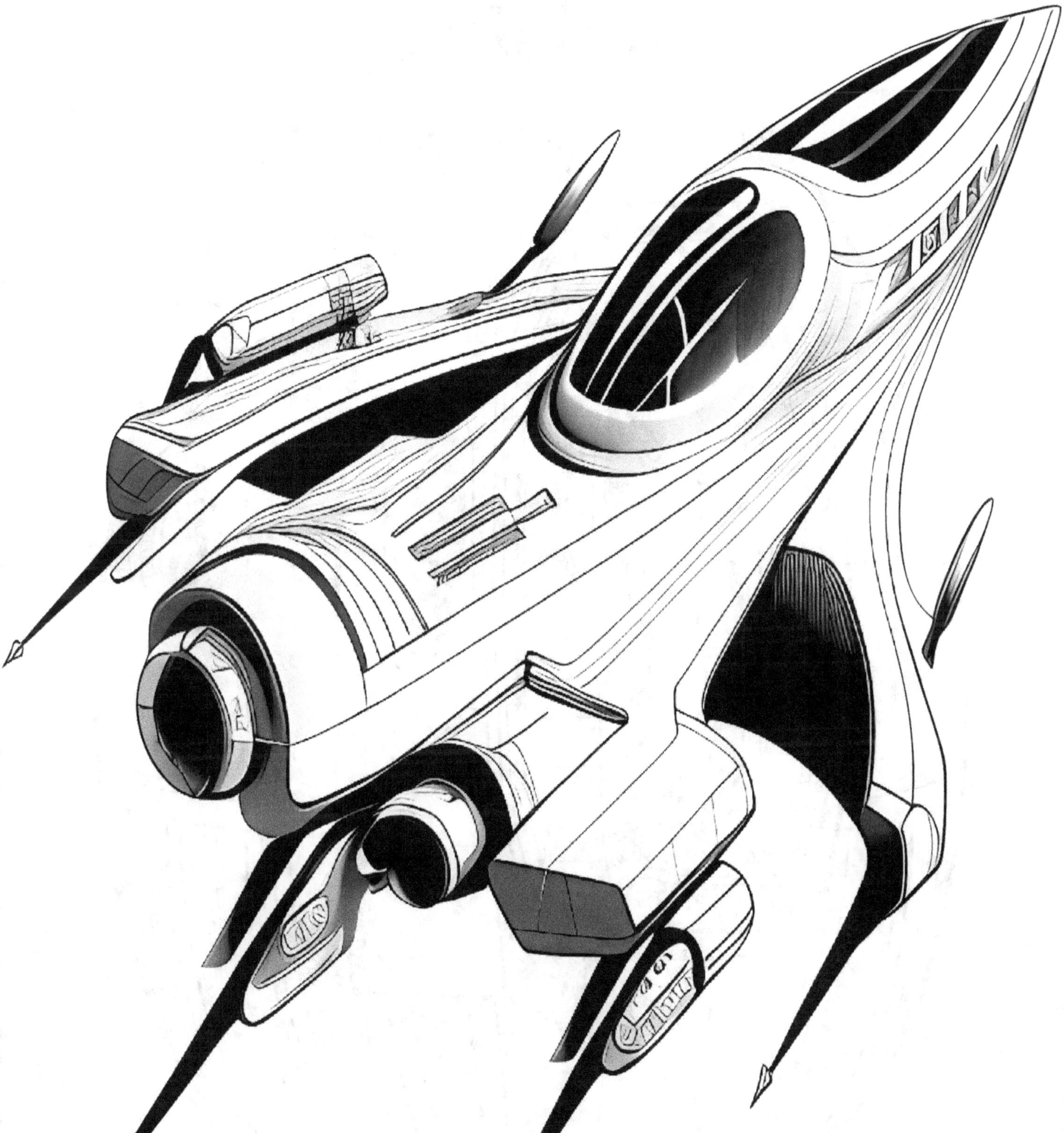

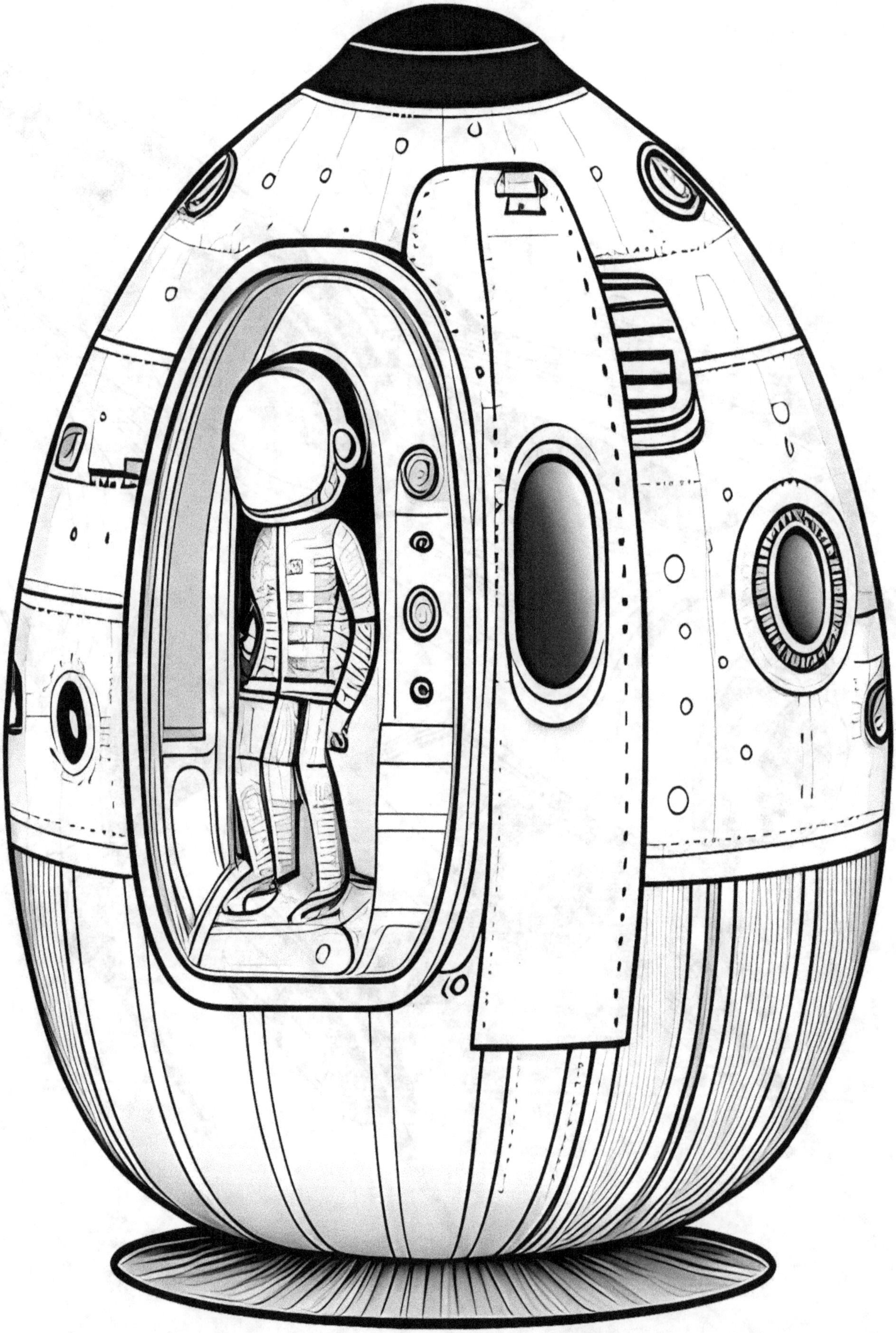

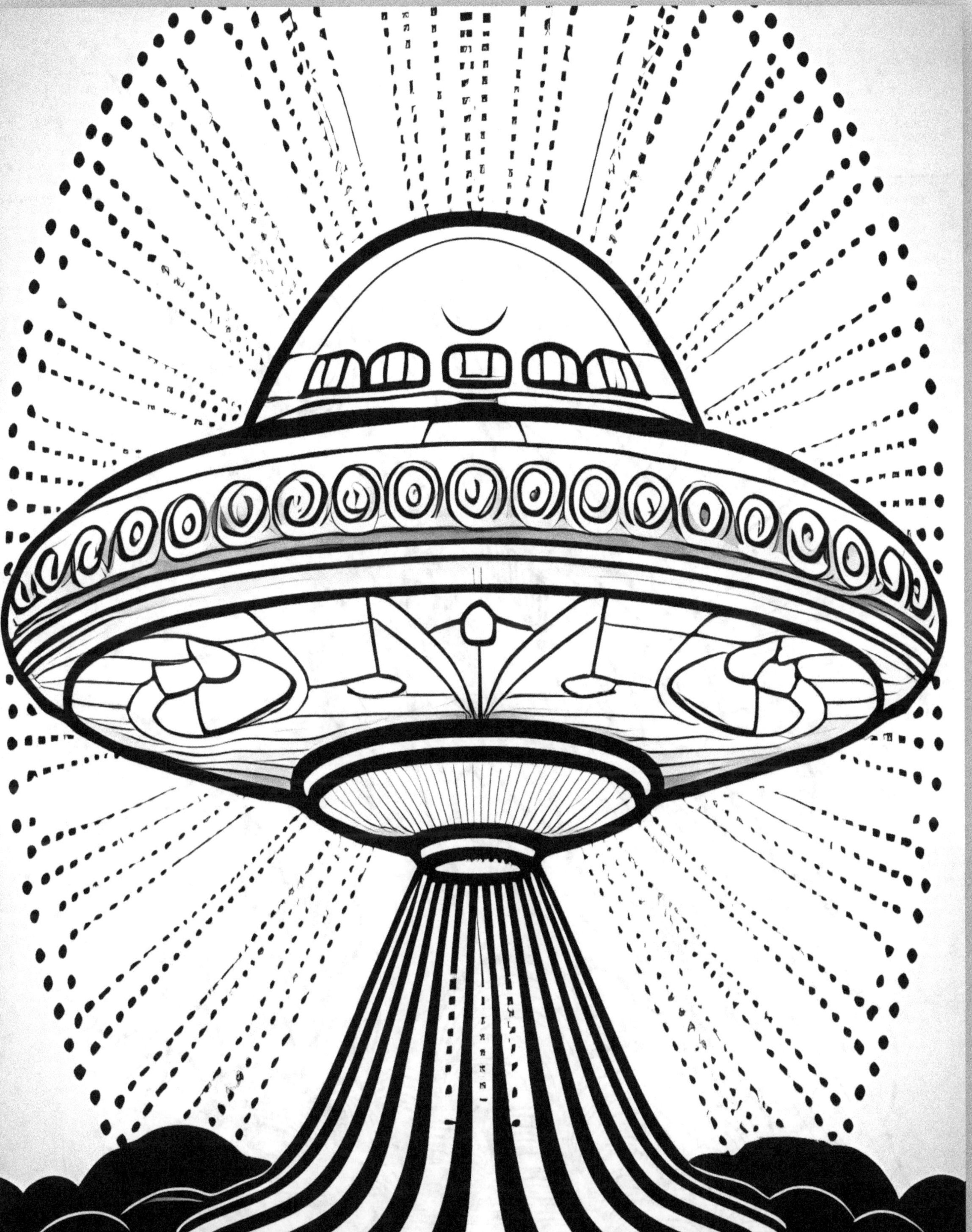

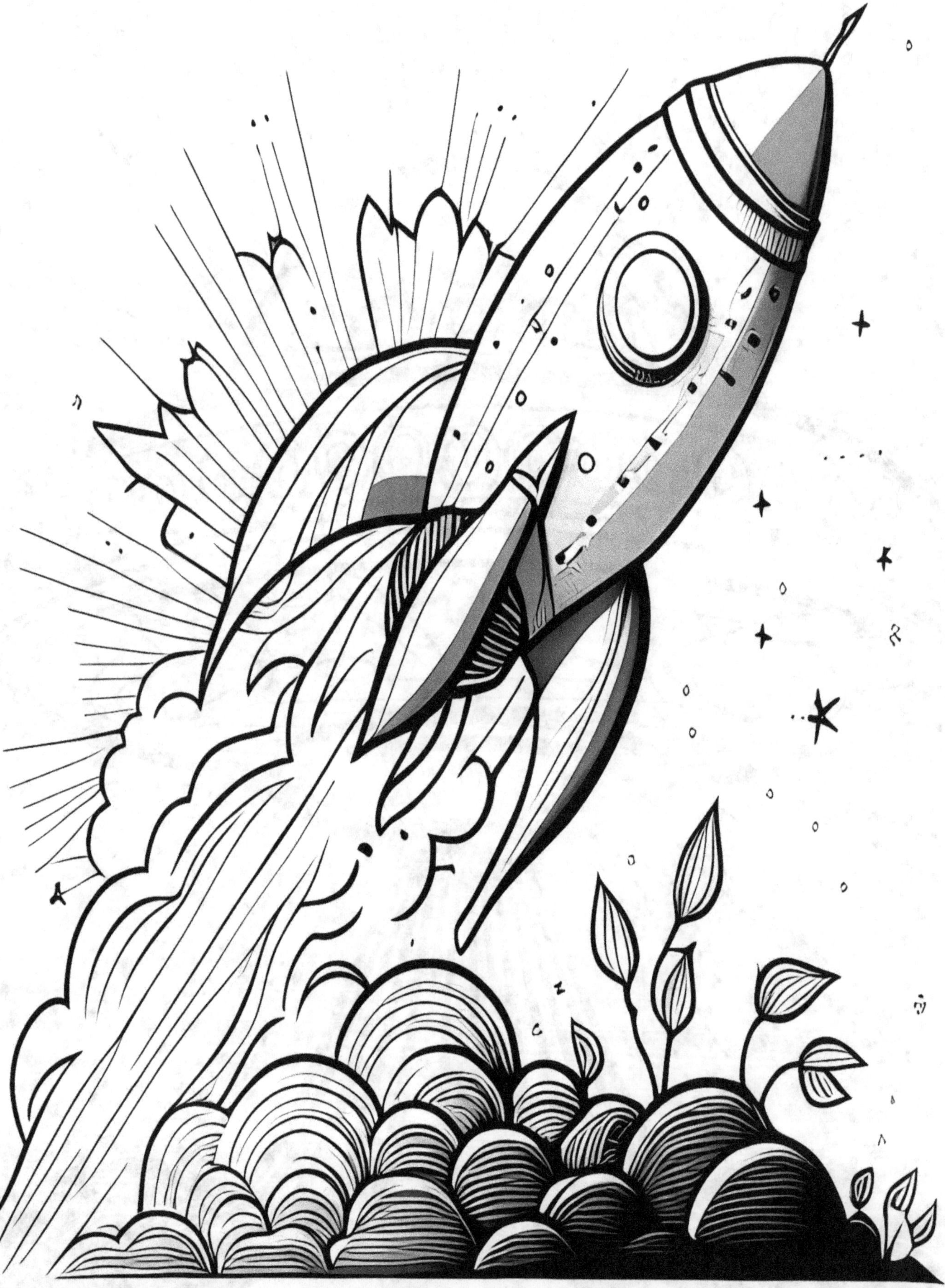

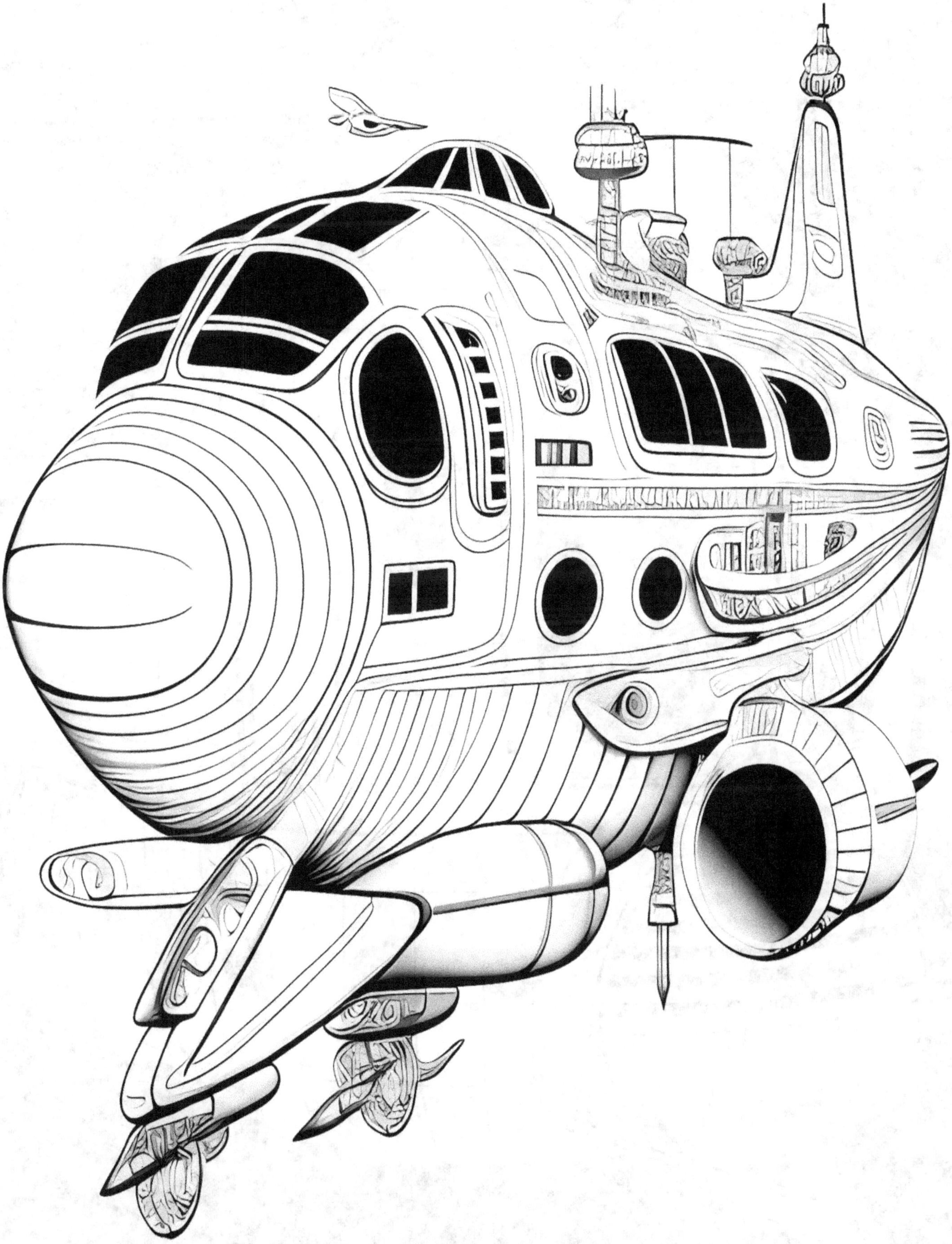

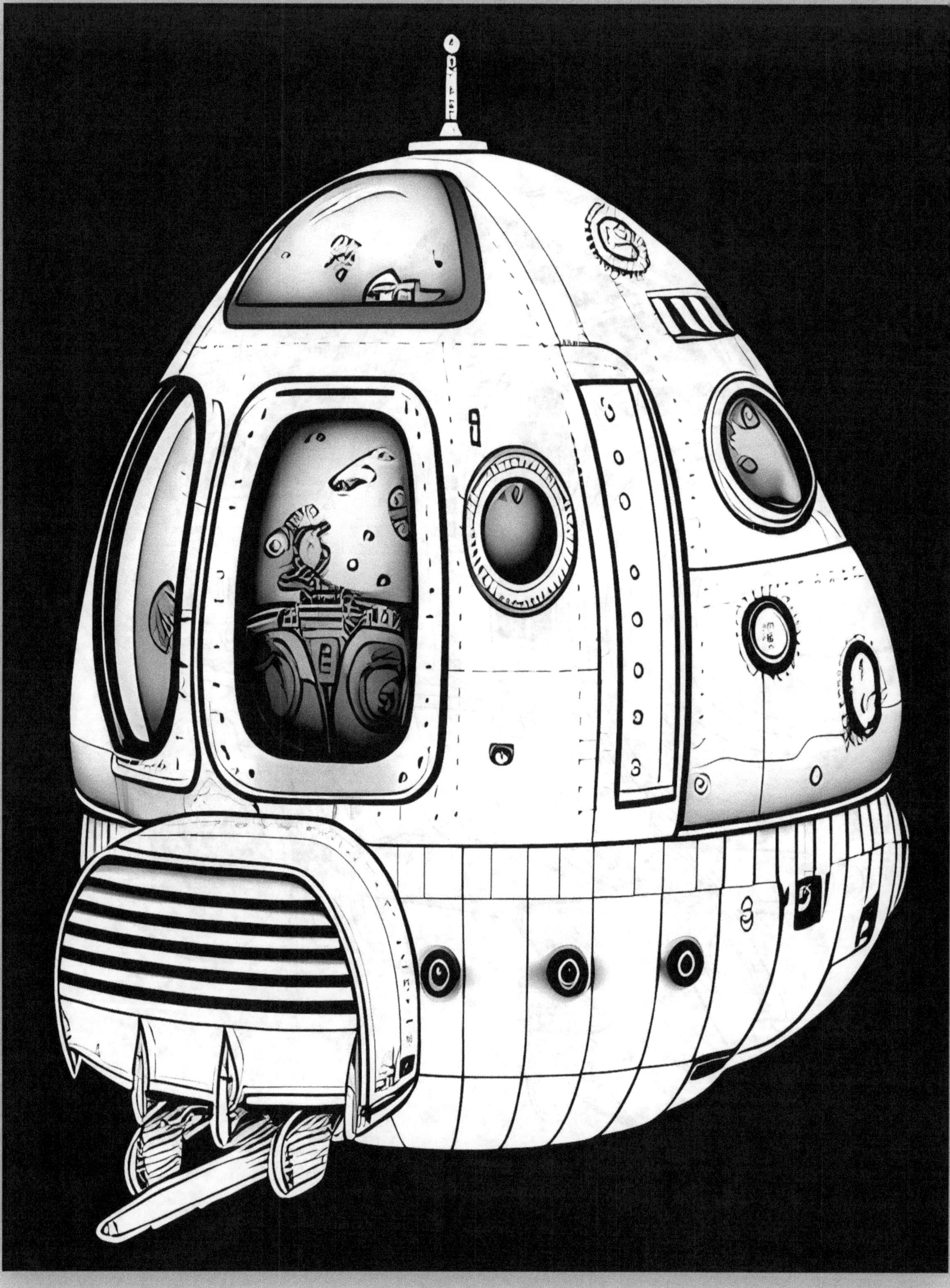

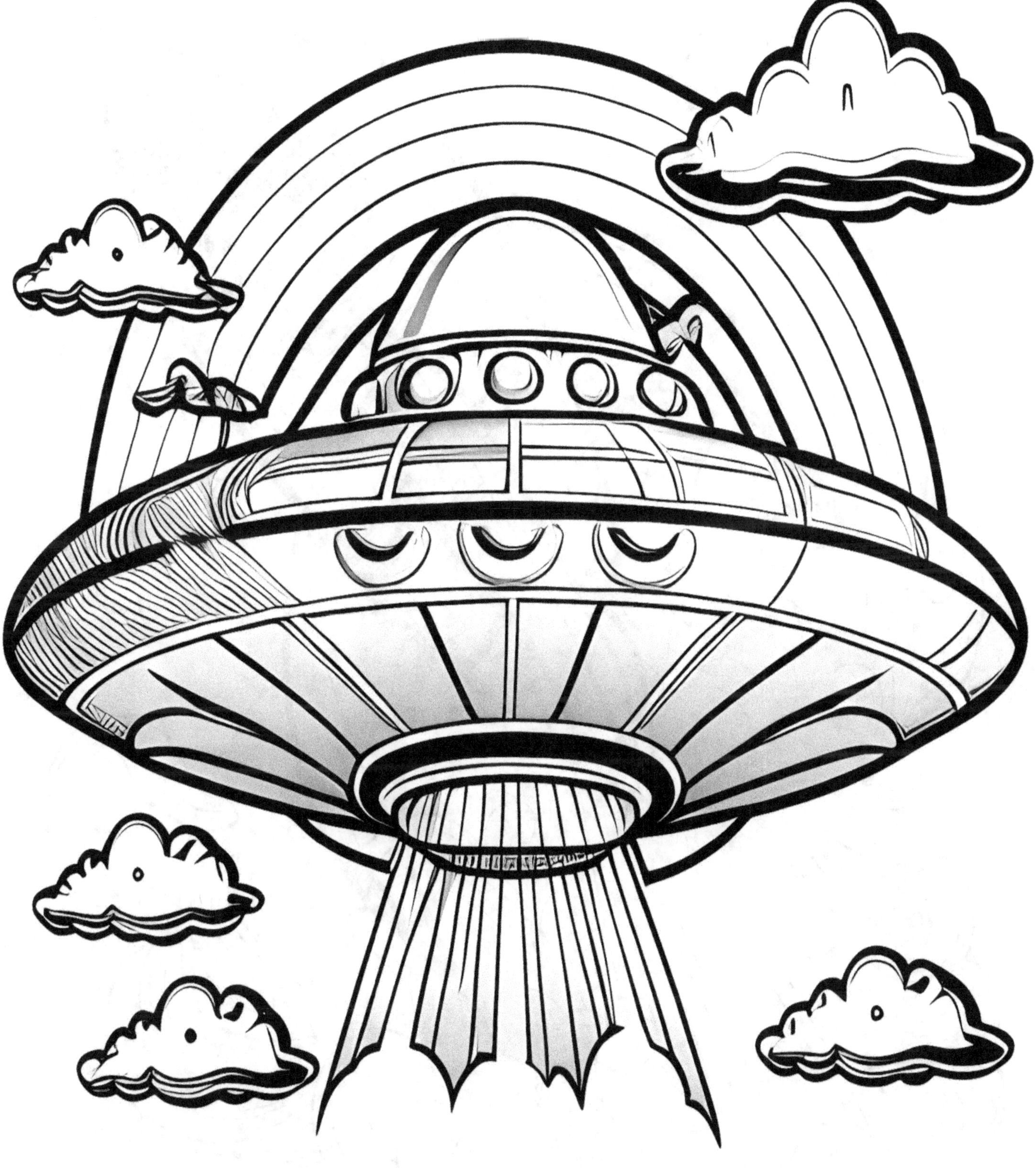

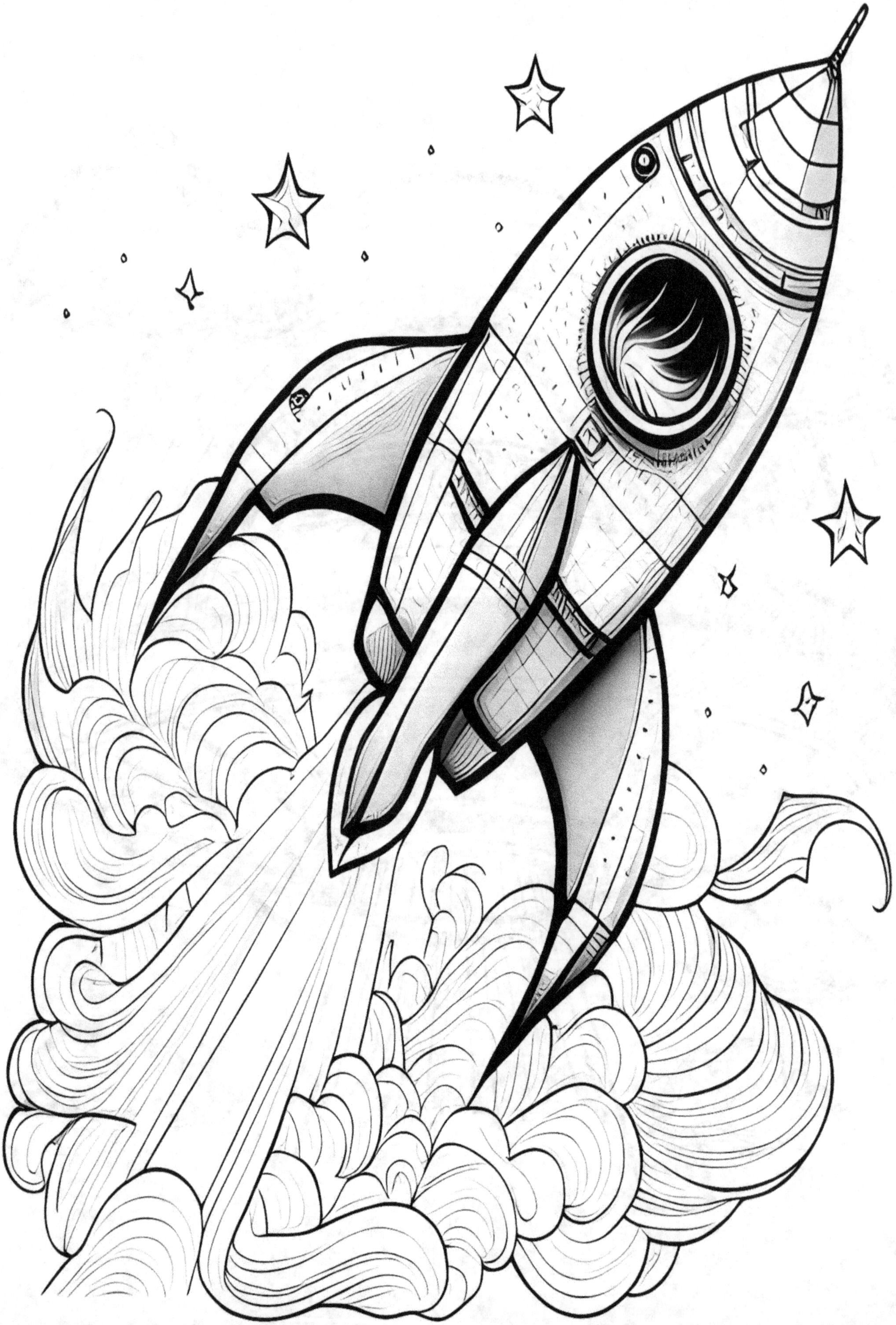

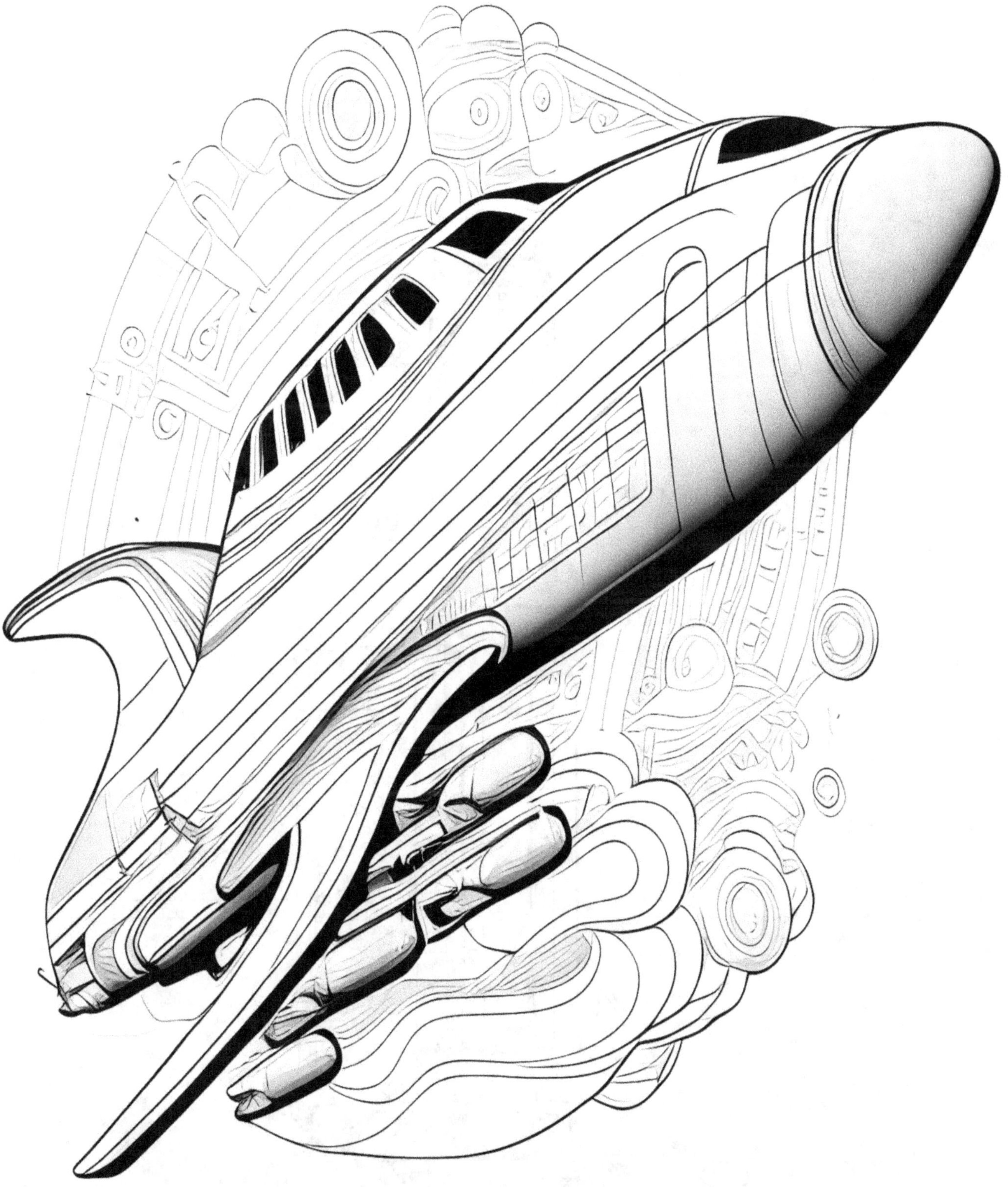

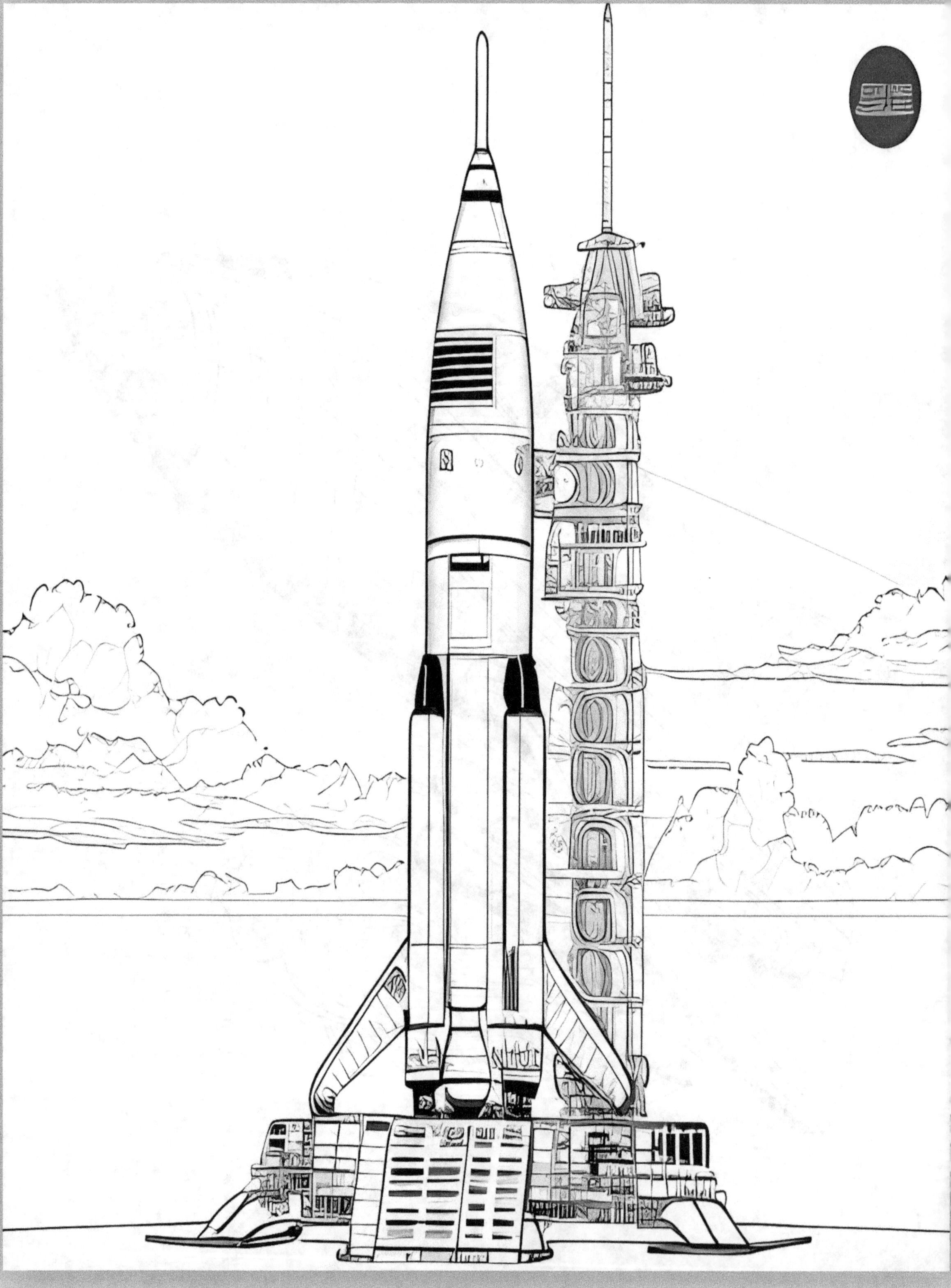

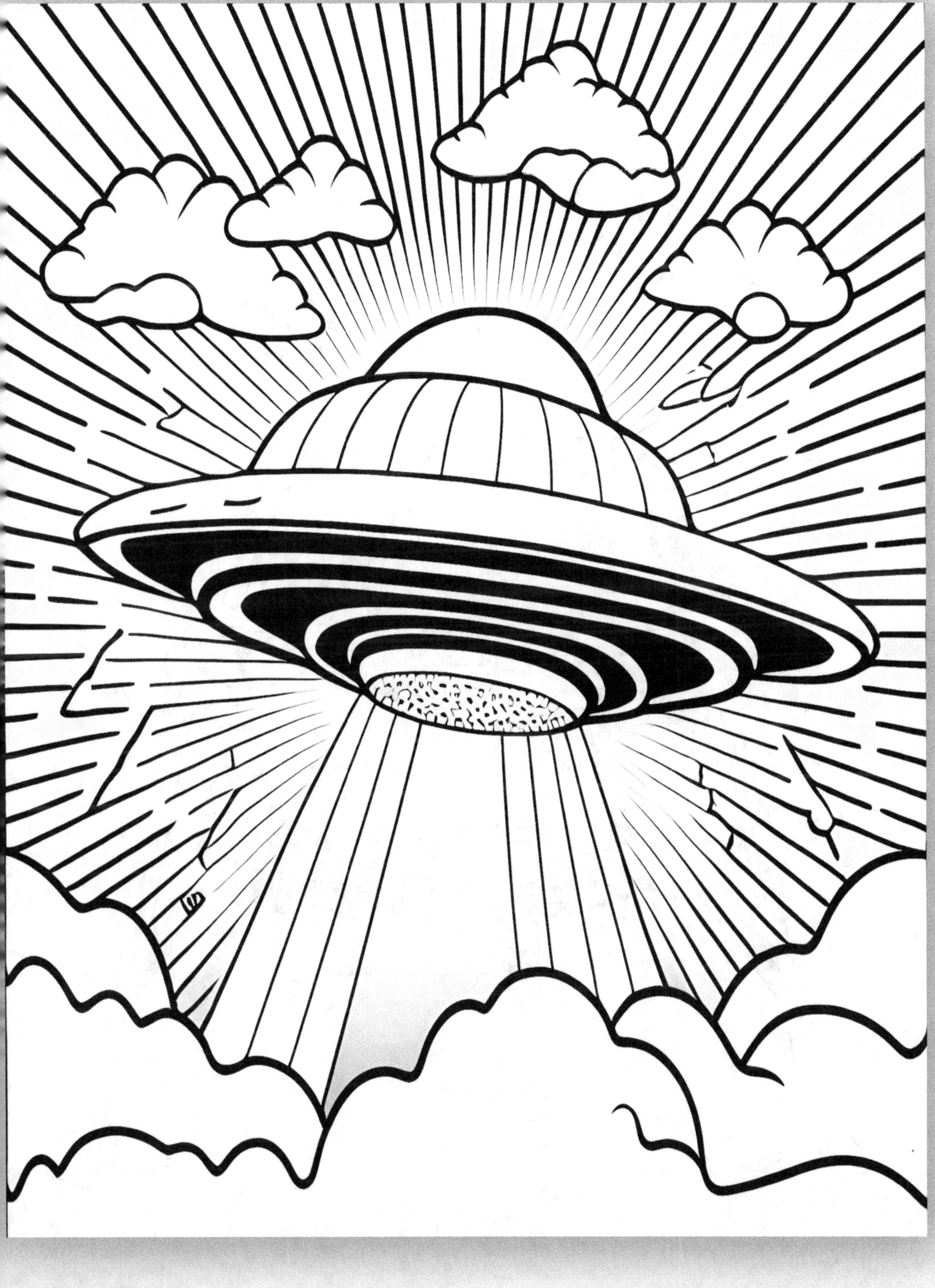

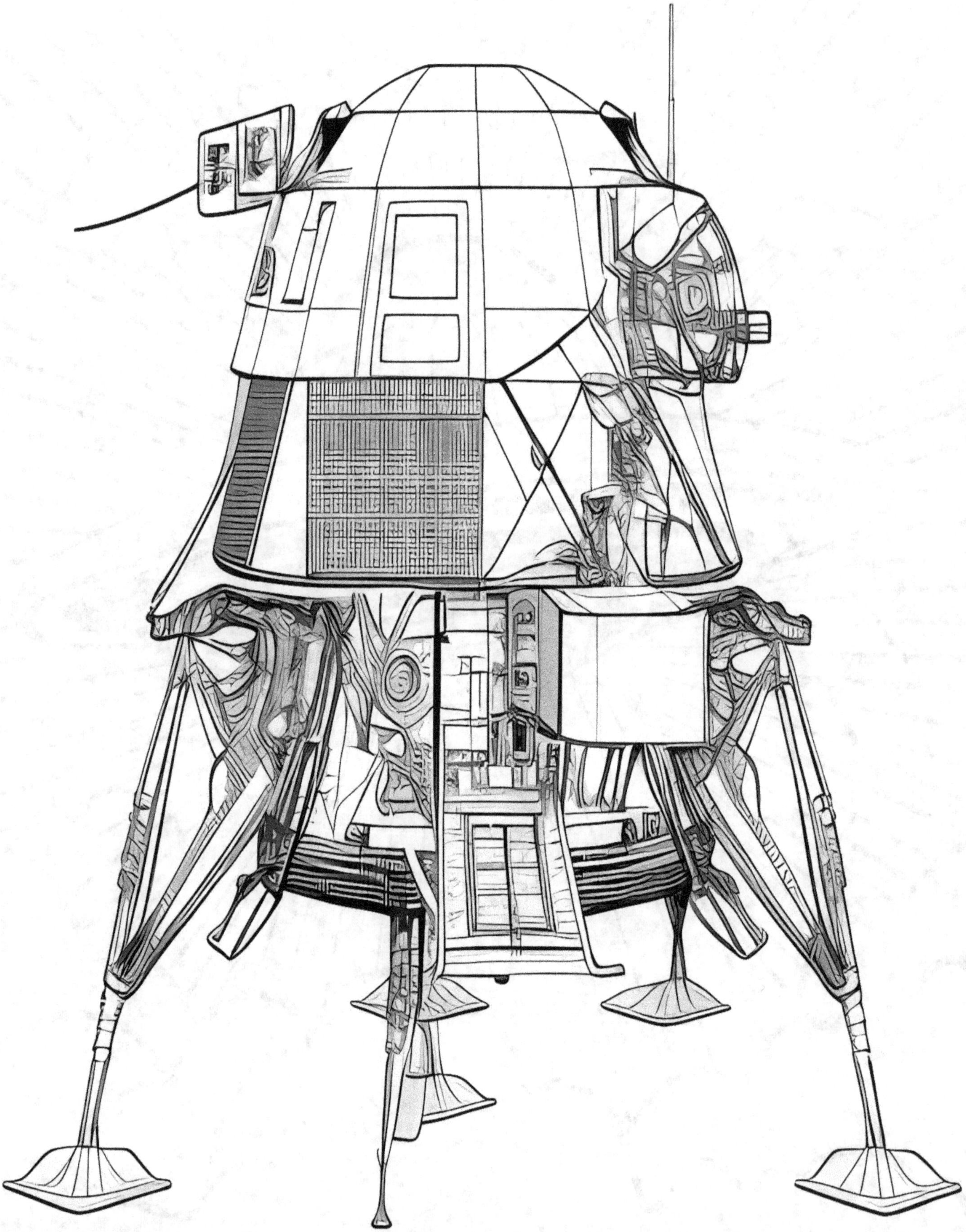

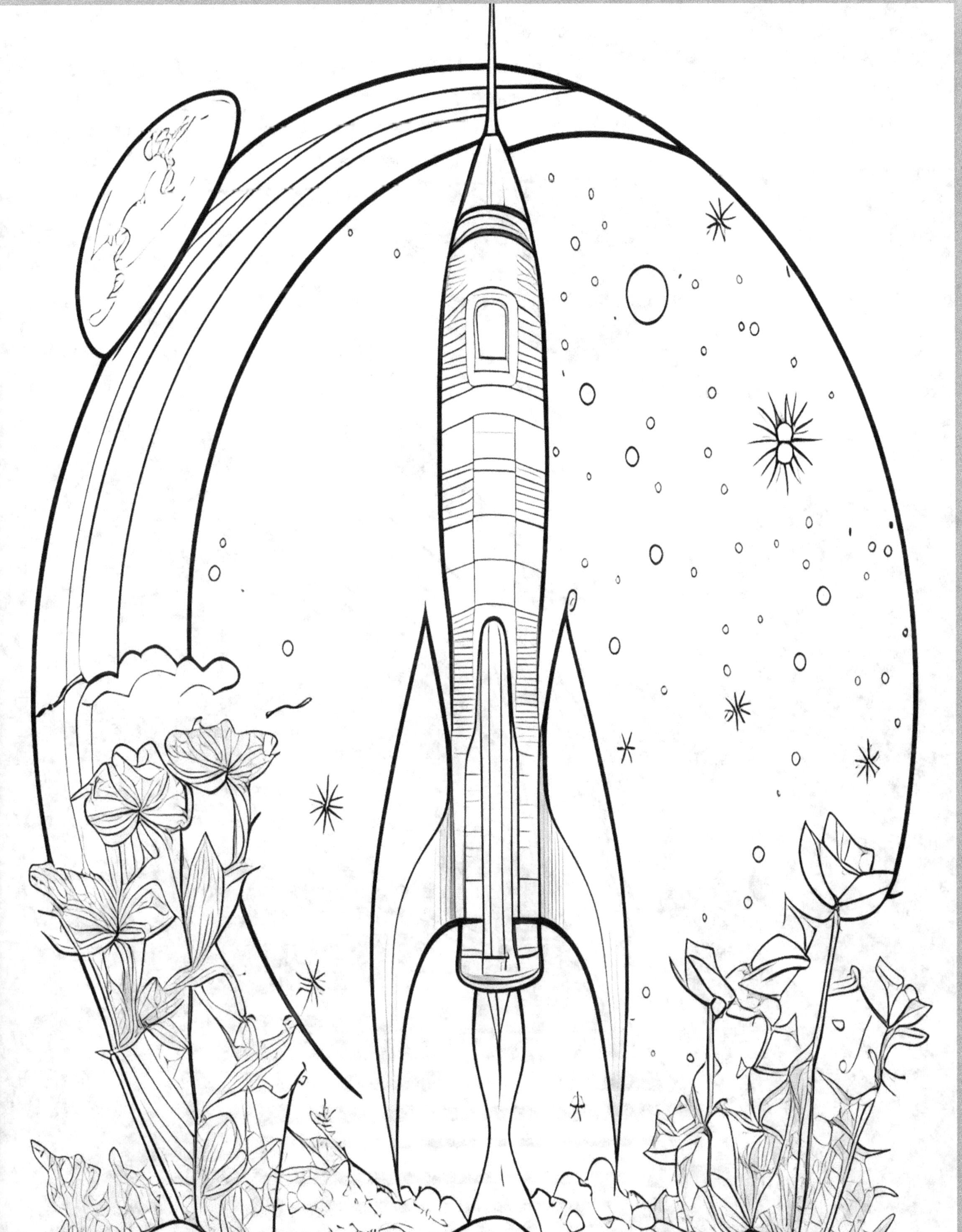

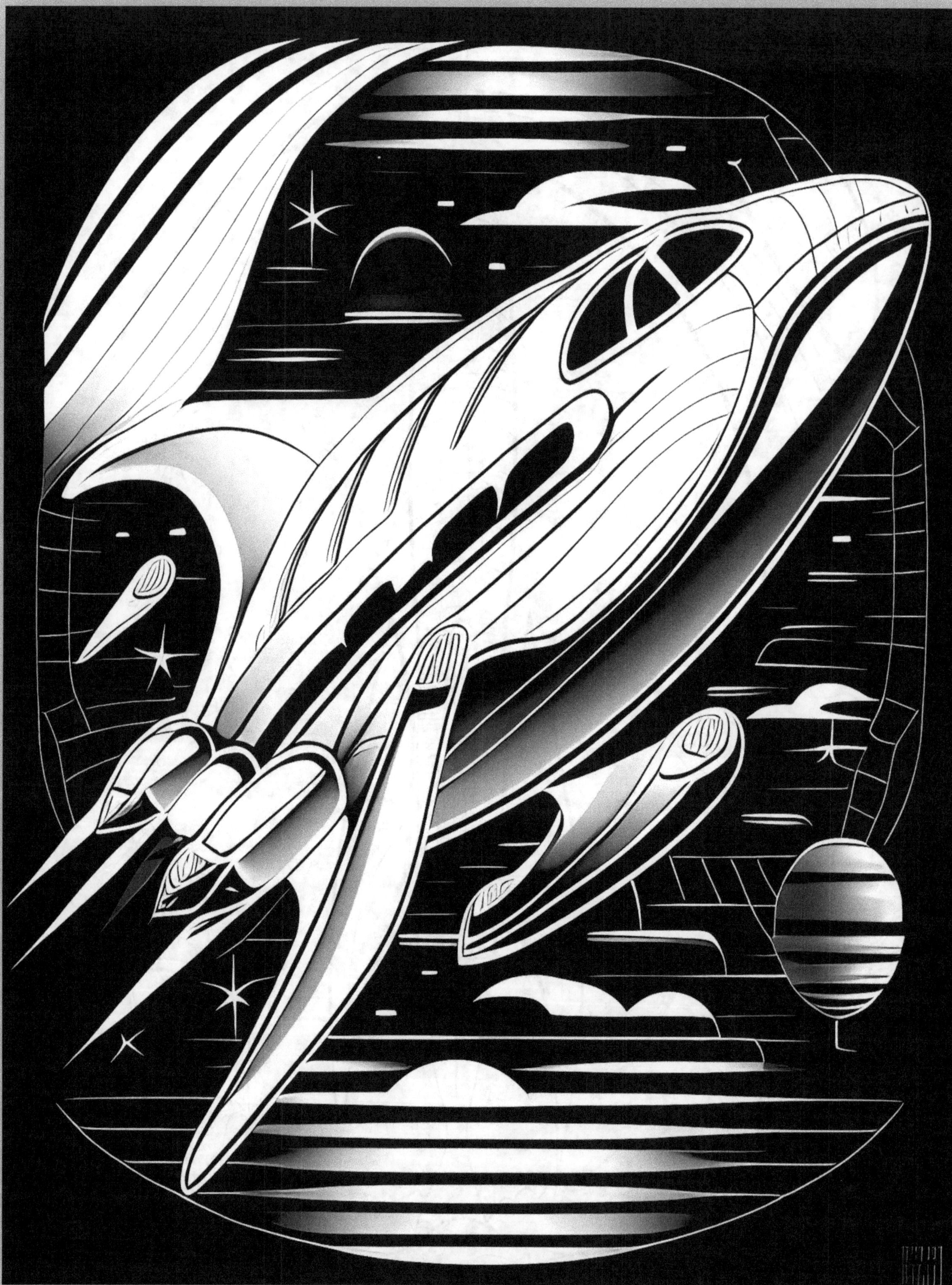

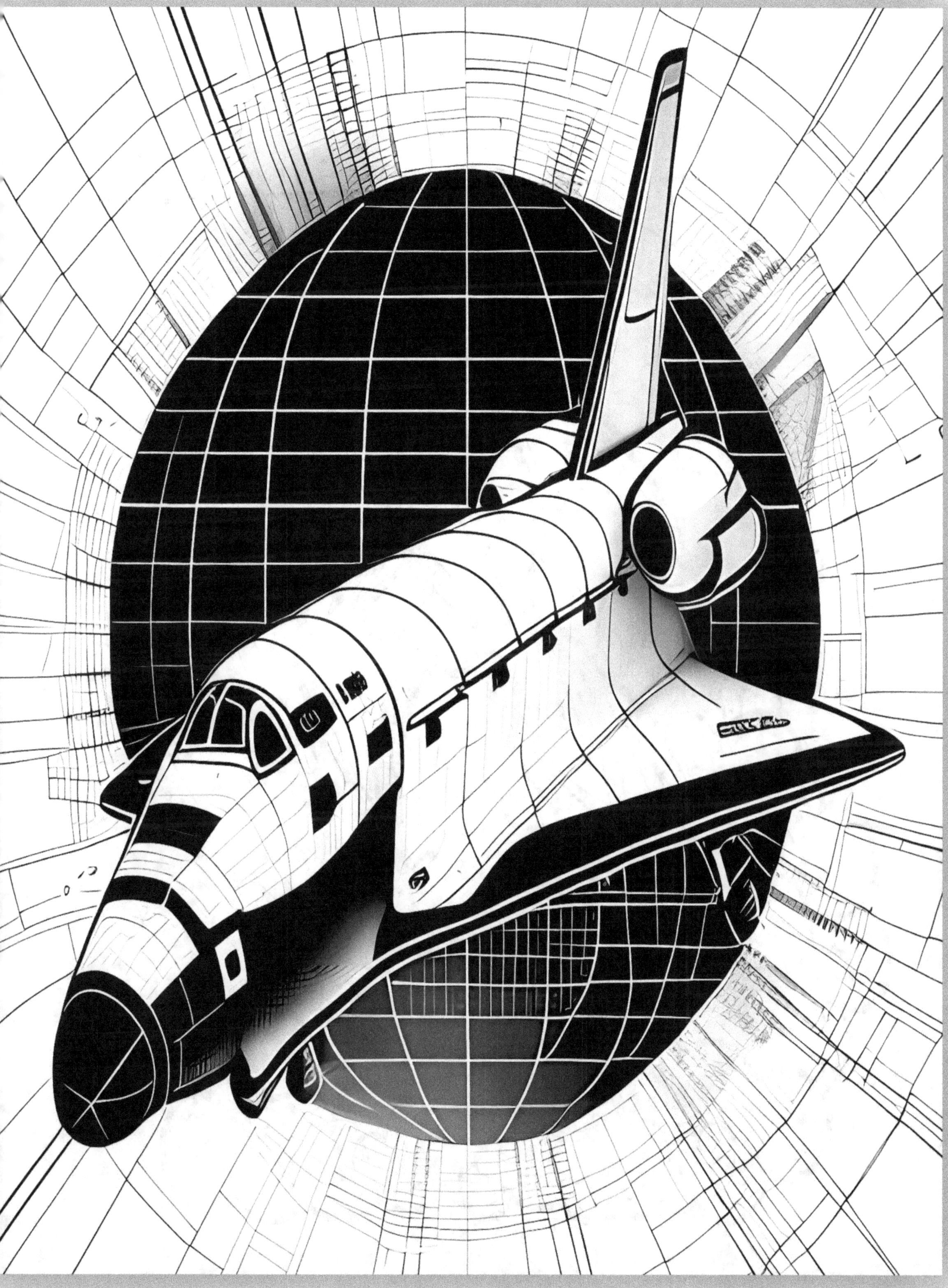

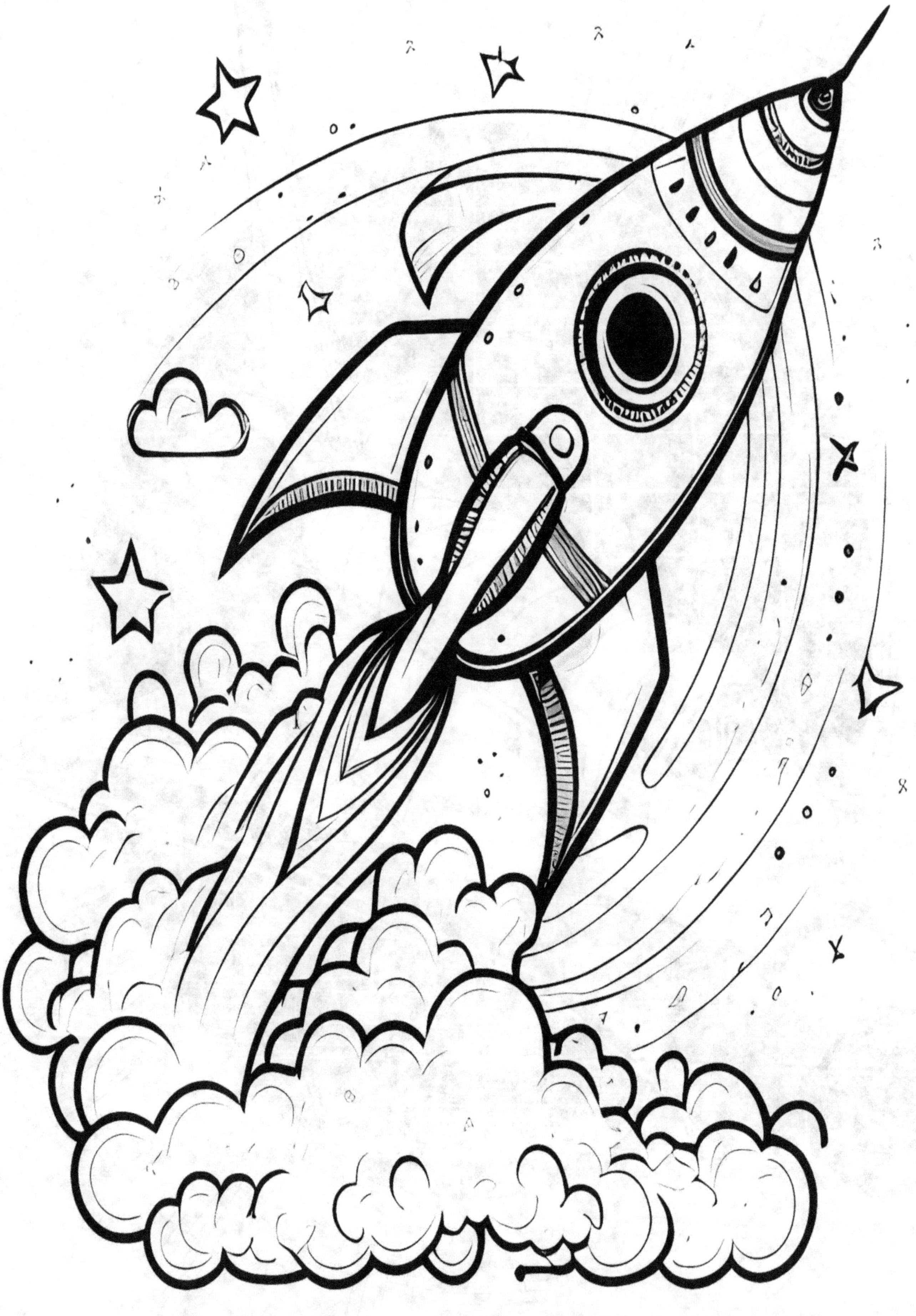

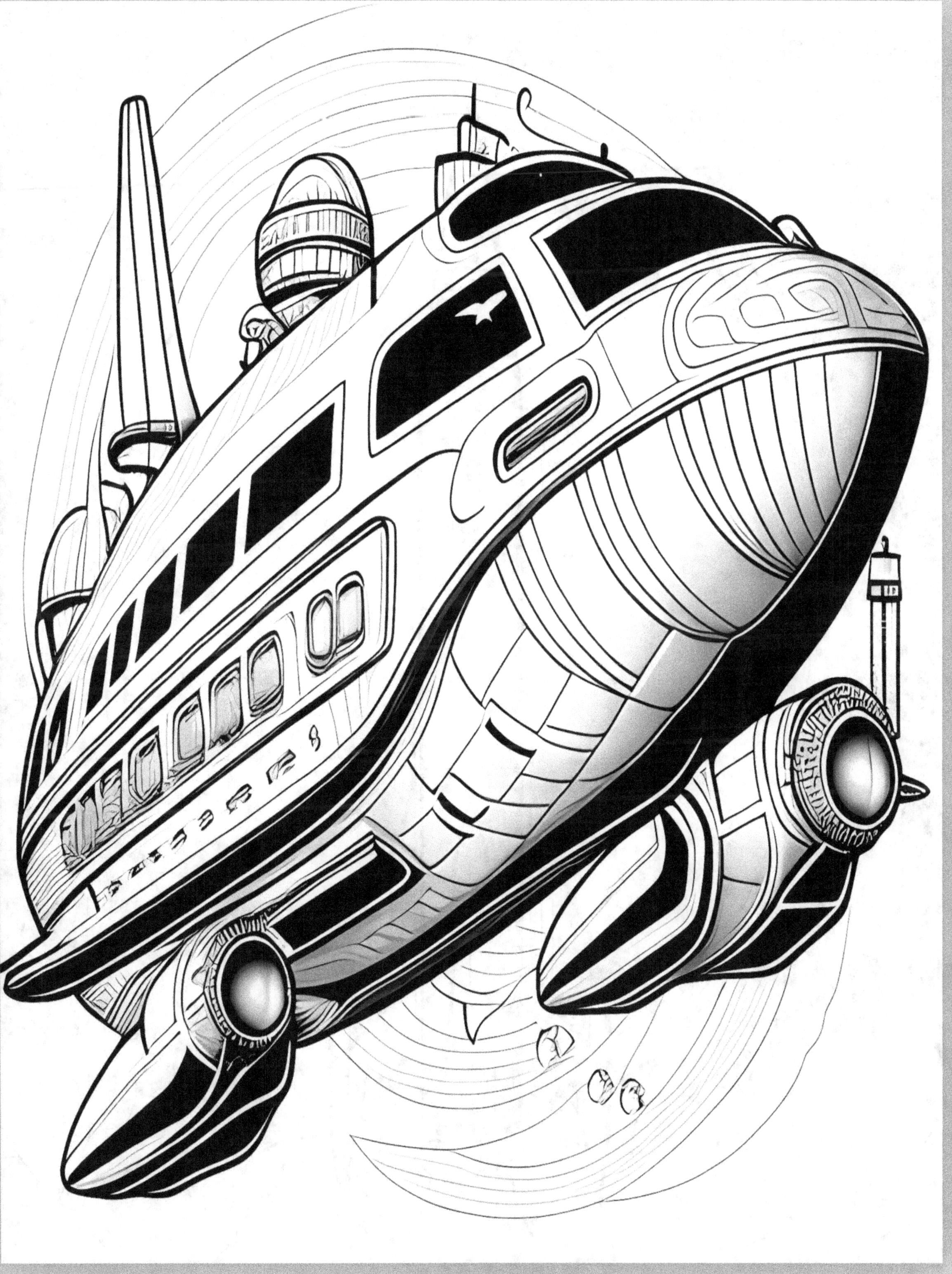

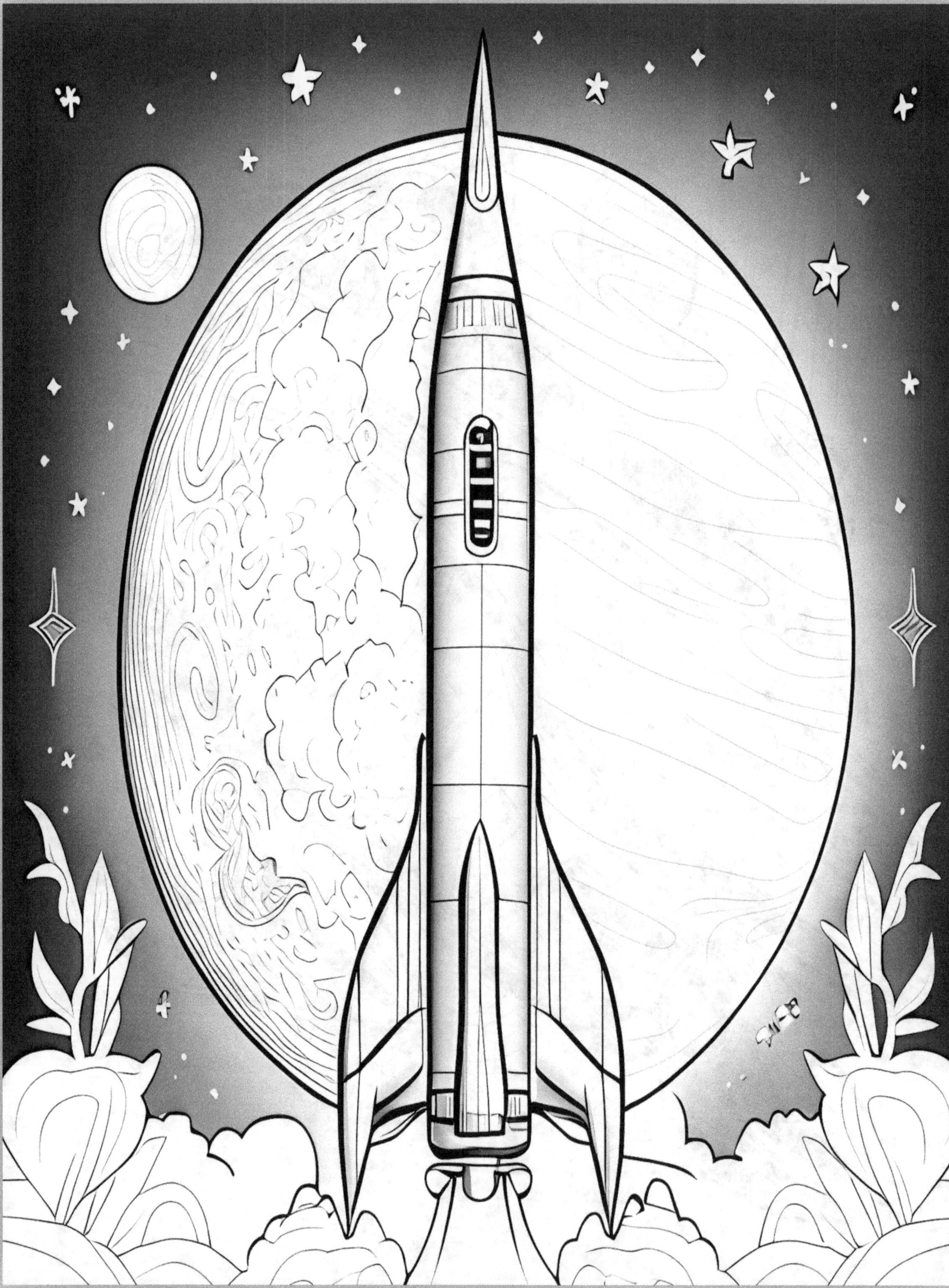

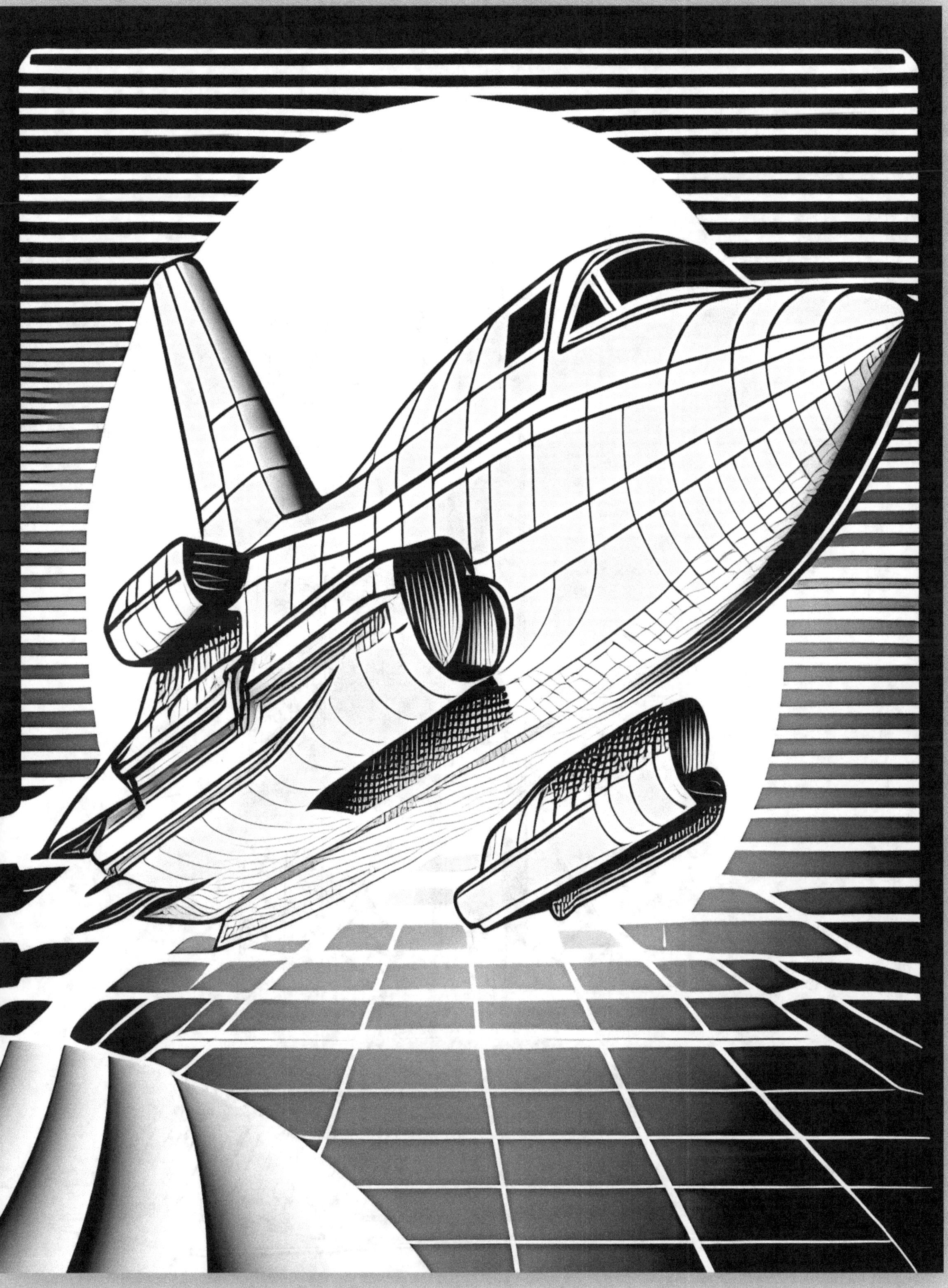

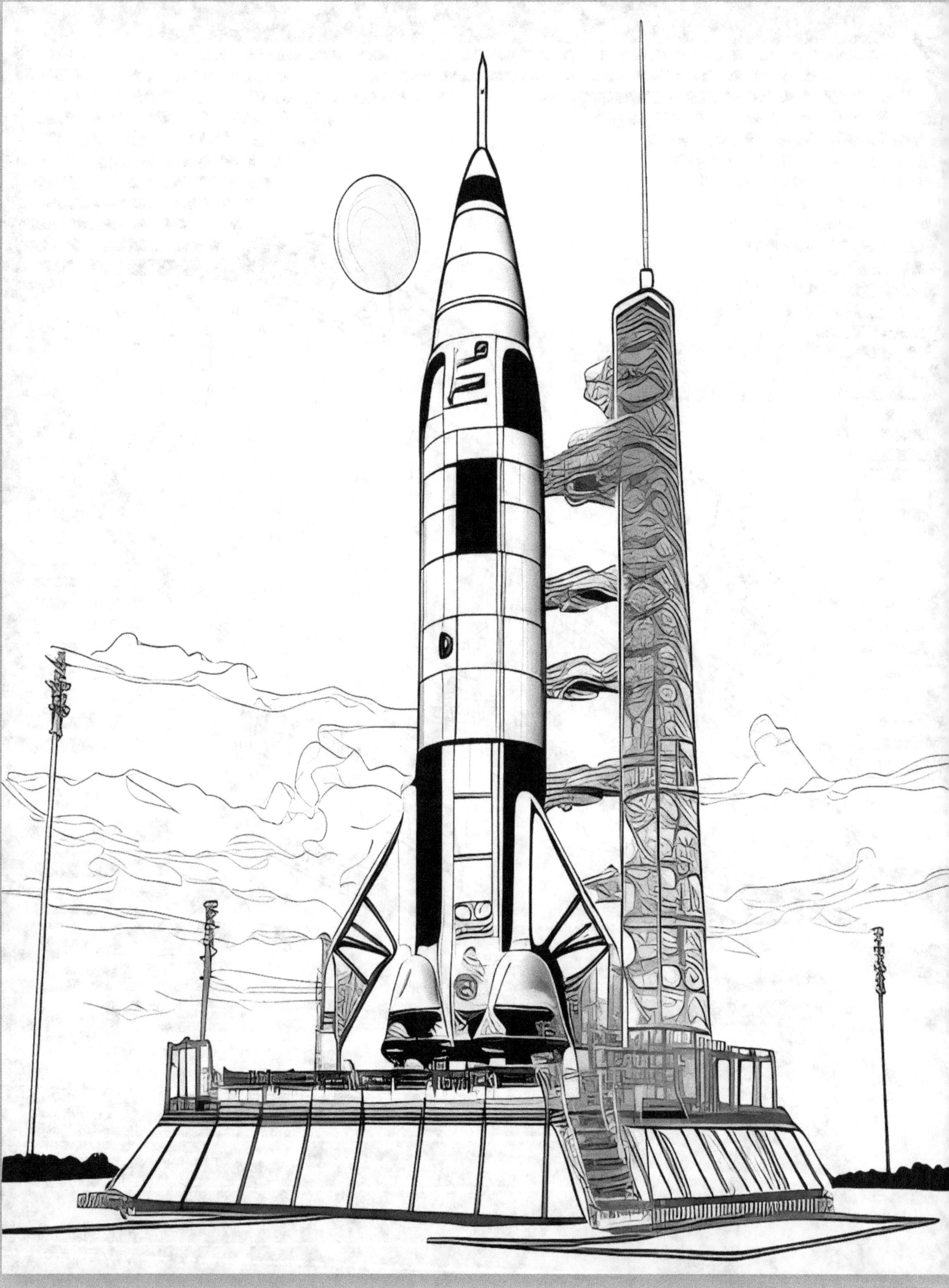

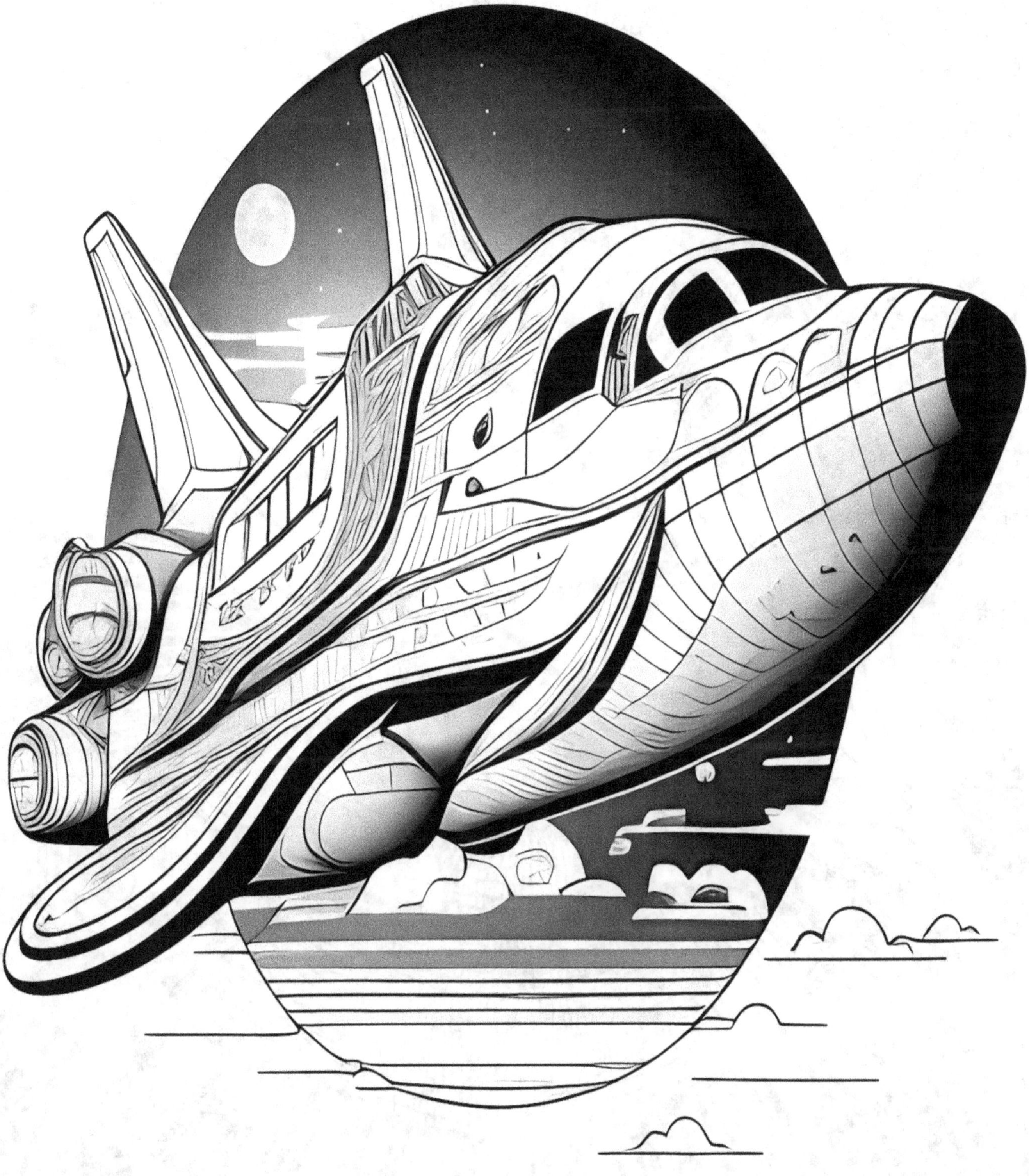

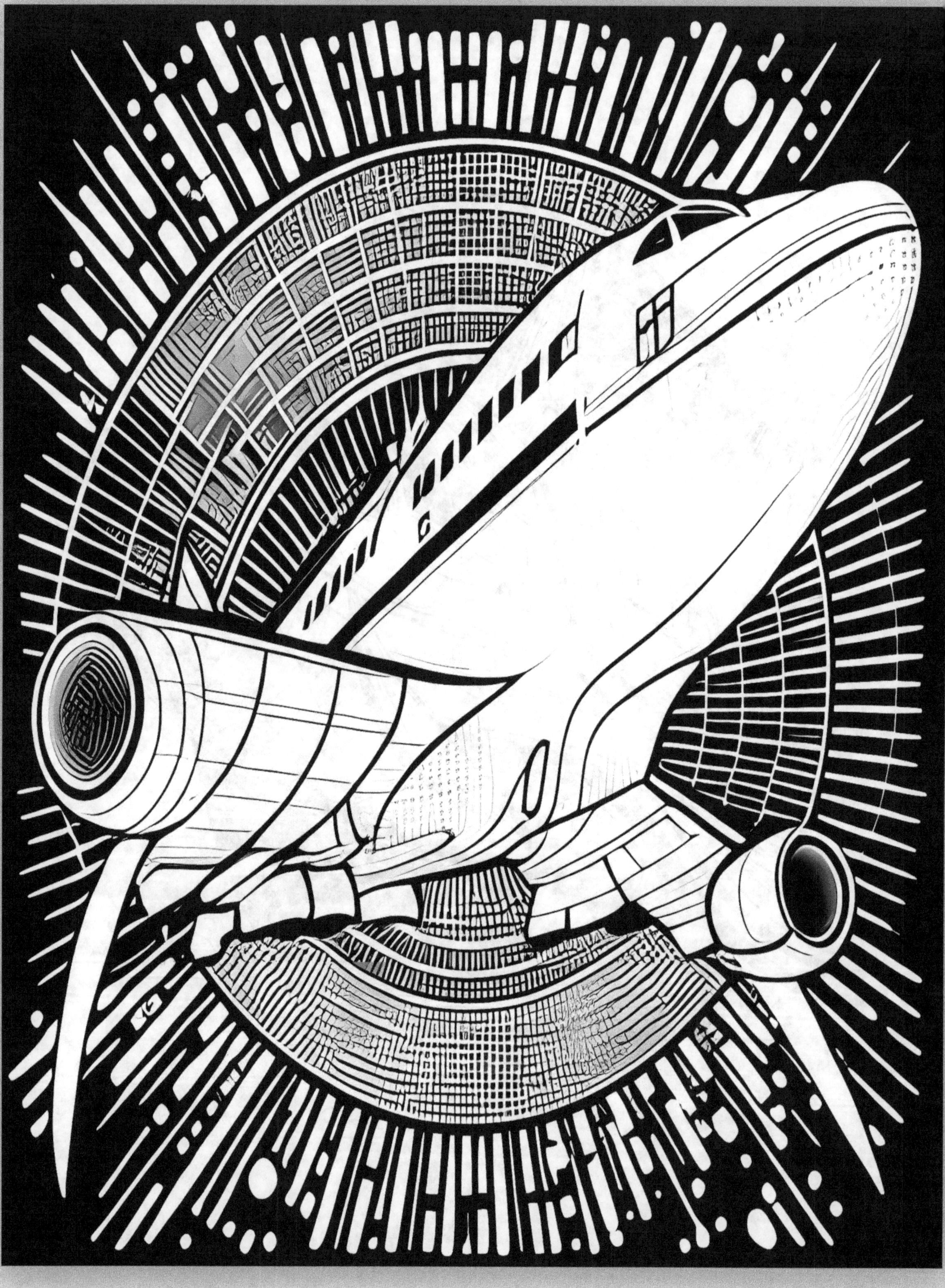

www.ingramcontent.com/pod-product-compliance
Lightning Source LLC
Chambersburg PA
CBHW081542220526
45467CB00010B/3294
* 9 7 9 8 3 8 6 3 5 0 3 1 4 *